ESCAPE TO THE

Hawaiian
ISLANDS

Photography by Robert Holmes

Text by Paul Wood

FODOR'S TRAVEL PUBLICATIONS

NEW YORK • TORONTO • LONDON • SYDNEY • AUCKLAND • WWW.FODORS.COM

First Edition
ISBN 0-679-00798-9
ISSN 1531-3360

Special Sales

Fodor's Travel Publications are available at special discounts for bulk purchases for sales promotions or premiums. Special editions, including personalized covers, excerpts of existing guides, and corporate imprints, can be created in large quantities for special needs. For more information, contact your local bookseller or write to Special Markets, Fodor's Travel Publications, 280 Park Avenue, New York, NY 10017. Inquiries from Canada should be directed to your local Canadian bookseller or sent to Random House of Canada, Ltd., Marketing Dept., 2775 Matheson Boulevard East, Mississauga, Ontario L4W 4P7. Inquiries from the United Kingdom should be sent to Fodor's Travel Publications, 20 Vauxhall Bridge Road, London, England SW1V 2SA.

PRINTED IN THE UNITED STATES OF AMERICA
10 9 8 7 6 5 4 3 2 1

Acknowledgments

The writer heartily thanks Aloha Airlines for its generosity (and dependability); also the good people in each island's visitors bureau—especially Charlene Kauhane of the Maui Visitors Bureau. But that's not all. This book is really a gift to you made by the people of Hawai'i, who said "yes" wholeheartedly to our hundreds of requests. *Aloha kakou.*

From Robert Holmes: A special thanks to my daughters, Emma and Hannah, and my wife, Bobbie, who tolerated my long absences when I found it difficult to pretend I was spending another long, hard day at the office. To my parents, Maurice and Marjorie Holmes, who encouraged me to explore the world at an early age. And not least, a huge thanks to Fabrizio La Rocca, whose passion and exceptional support made this book a reality.

Credits

Creative Director and Series Editor: Fabrizio La Rocca
Editorial Director: Karen Cure
Art Director: Tigist Getachew

Editors: Jennifer Paull, Candice Gianetti
Editorial Production: Linda Schmidt
Production/Manufacturing: C.R. Bloodgood, Robert B. Shields
Maps: David Lindroth, Inc.

Most books on the travel shelves are either long on the nitty-gritty and short on evocative photographs, or the other way around. We at Fodor's think that the different balance in this slim volume is just perfect, rather like the intersection of the most luscious magazine article and a sensible, down-to-earth guidebook. On the road, the useful pages at the end of the book are practically all you need. For the planning, roam through the color photographs up front. Each one reveals a key facet of the corner of the Hawaiian Islands it portrays, and taken together with the lyrical accompanying text, all convey a sense of place that will take you there before you go. Each page opens up one of Hawai'i's most exceptional experiences; each spread leads you to the quintessential places that highlight the islands' spirit at its purest.

Some of these experiences are sure to beckon. You may hike through the green, mysterious realm of a bamboo forest, bathe under the lacy 400-foot veil of Waimoku Falls, glide over the crowded underwater reefs of Hanauma Bay, or feel your senses reawaken among the flowers crowded in stands at Hilo's farmers' market. You may ride turquoise waves or dusty cattle trails, teeter on the edge of gigantic seaside cliffs, or travel back in time as you explore the simple life of Japanese coffee farmers. Or, wrapped in a blanket, the early morning sun in your eyes, squinting and shivering, gaze in awe at an immense crater that you will soon descend.

To capture the raw energy of these islands, photographer Robert Holmes stepped on still-hot, newly created land in Hawai'i Volcanoes National Park, where the primordial elements meet when lava reaches the sea. It was, he says, "the experience of seeing the Earth as it was at creation." Writer Paul Wood's intimate relationship with Hawai'i is grounded in his almost electromagnetic attraction to a mountain, Haleakalā; his certainty that the old gods have not passed from the Earth; and his bemused affection for all true Hawaiians, whatever their ethnic origins.

Follow in the footsteps of Holmes and Wood, and you too will get a sense of the ancient soul of these islands. Be prepared to embrace their natural forces, their sharp contrasts, and their boundless energy. Forget your projects and deadlines. And escape to the Hawaiian Islands. You owe it to yourself.

—The Editors

MOST MORNINGS IN HAWAI'I FIND YOU HEADING FOR THE BEACH, but today you're staring down into a big hole in the ground. Heat pulses from the glowing stones that line the bottom, and you feel a warning burn on your face when you step too close. No, this is not the crater of a waking volcano but, rather, the heart of the islands' traditional ultimate celebration: the lū'au. As men lower banana-tree trunks, then a layer of ti leaves, into the *imu,* or pit oven, a burst of nutty, vegetal-smelling steam rushes up. The prepared pig is stretched out on the green bed, covered with more leaves and trunks—and more foods for roasting. On top go wet sacks, a clean sheet; then the whole assemblage is smothered with earth to keep every bit of steam within. At sunset you're back, a lei

Live Like a Hawaiian

LŪ'AU, LAHAINA, MAUI

Though limited to the natural elements—water and wind, stone and fire—and the bounty of the earth they revered, the ancient Hawaiians really knew how to throw a party.

around your neck and the faint impression of a greeting kiss on your cheek. The electrified band is playing "Funky Hula Girl." Then, in a wink, the wraps come off the imu—a gesture of magnificent prosperity—and a savory blast erupts from the earth. The pig is dumped into a trough, and the shredders attack it, flashing their long forks. The rest of the feast—the stew "chicken lū'au," little ti-leaf-wrapped meat bundles called *laulau*—is spread across a communal table: there's enough food for a small village, so a village must gather. You find a seat and dig in. The tender pork tastes dark and rich. Other flavors are strange at first, but they all work together, harmonizing with the smell of smoke from the pit. Now the party's in full swing, complete with fire-tossers, perhaps, and dancers who kick, spin, and yelp. Maybe you'll want to get up and dance, too. It's only natural—a lū'au turns everyone into a Hawaiian.

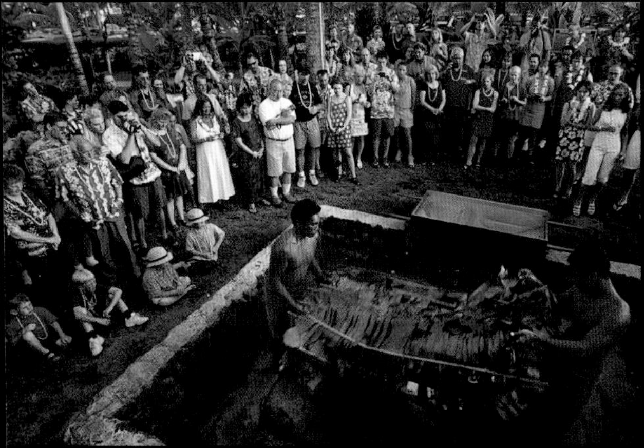

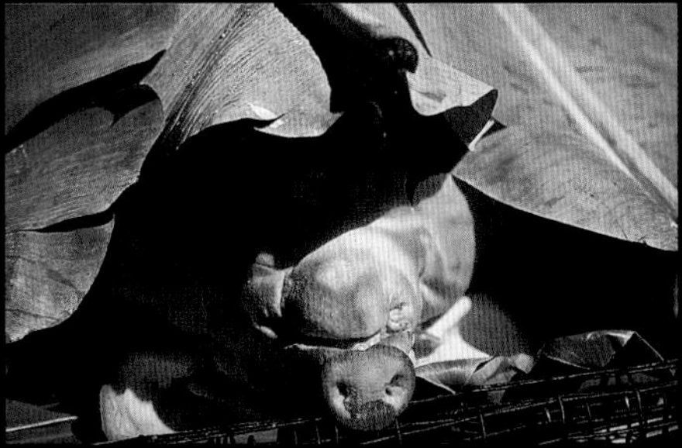

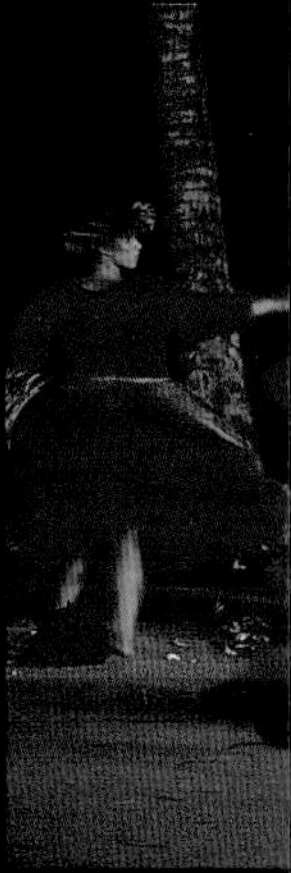

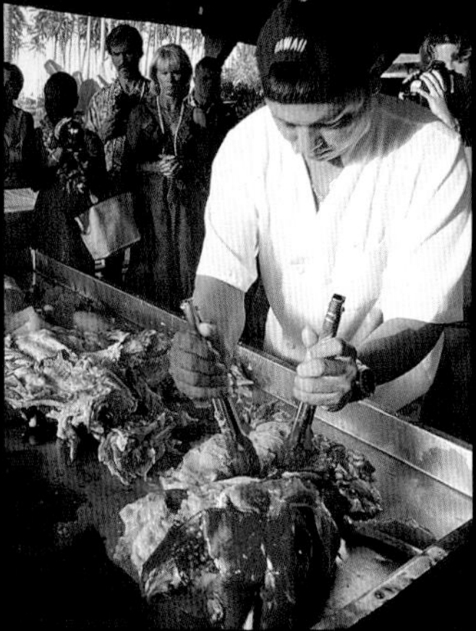

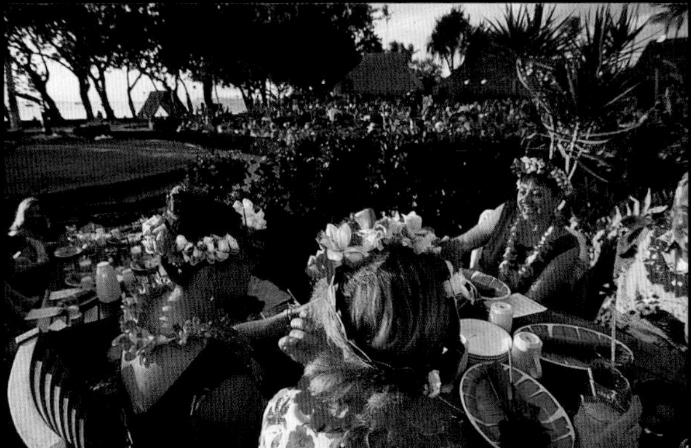

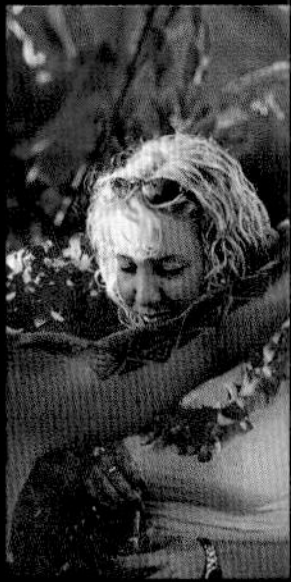

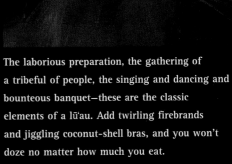

The laborious preparation, the gathering of a tribeful of people, the singing and dancing and bounteous banquet—these are the classic elements of a lū'au. Add twirling firebrands and jiggling coconut-shell bras, and you won't doze no matter how much you eat.

THE FISH OF HANAUMA BAY LIVE LIKE ROYALTY; for that they have Elvis to thank. His 1961 movie *Blue Hawaii* burned images of cliff-ringed Hanauma into the popular imagination, and it quickly became the top snorkeling spot in Hawai'i. As the fish immediately realized, snorkelers sometimes provide handouts. Today the 100-acre bay supports far more sea life than nature alone could possibly sustain. Of course, not even the King could have created this phenomenon on his own—the pristine bay deserves most of the credit. Just after the road east from Honolulu narrows to a single, coast-hugging scenic route, the perfect crescent of Hanauma comes into view, its intense blues turning gradually from the palest turquoise to a lustrous cobalt. Even from the road you can see the silvery streaks

A Floating World

HANAUMA BAY, KOKO HEAD, O'AHU

Gazing through your strap-on window into the crowded communities of the reefs, you can't help but feel that Hawai'i's underwater wonders equal those above.

of chubs, jacks, surgeonfish, butterfly fishes—all streaming after the snorkelers. Park at the cliff-top lot and pad down the steep path to the beach, squeeze your feet into a pair of fins, and slide into the cool, glassy waters of this gigantic, interactive tropical-fish tank. Getting horizontal, you gaze down into the crowded communities of the reefs. The fish accept your voyeuristic presence with apparent calm. The more you look, the more you notice: an eel pokes its grouchy head out of a cave; fluorescent urchins slowly wave their spines; a cleaner wrasse works his "barber shop," nibbling the parasites off any fish who stops by. Holding your breath, you angle down among the coral heads as a swarm of Moorish idols rises around you, fluttering like dancers' hands. A blue parrotfish chews on coral with his horny beak, then darts away, flicking up a small cloud of sand. Six feet below, a rare green sea turtle, big as a tabletop, swims by, flippers waving like wings. Fully submerged now into his world, you fly along after him.

The Tallest Mountain on Earth

SUMMIT, MAUNA KEA, HAWAI'I

YOUR FIRST MOMENTS ON TOP OF MAUNA KEA ARE LITERALLY BREATHTAKING. YOU STEP OUT OF THE car and into the shock of the altitude. Your lungs feel hungry. Your flesh tightens. The cold at 13,796 feet goes far beyond a familiar winter chill. When you turn to look back, the motion makes you dizzy. There are no plants in this volcanic landscape, just sharp brown clinkers heaped into hills. Mauna Kea's not the *highest* mountain on Earth, your guide explains, unless you measure from its base at the bottom of the Pacific—then it beats Everest by 4,000 feet. Around you are the immense domes of a dozen scattered observatories. Within these shining white-and-chrome curves, giant telescopes are being readied to stare into the night sky—for this is one of the world's best vantage points for watching the cosmos. Panting in the meager air, you follow the guide to one of the observatories. Inside the silent cavern of steel, you climb a cold catwalk and inch along the skin of the dome, gawking

Astronomers here can view 90 percent of the night sky, from the North Pole to the Southern Cross. Now, as night arrives, so can you.

at the telescope, an awesome fusion of spikes and cylinders draped with heavy cable. Back outside, follow the trail to the summit, marked by a small wooden tower ornamented with foliage and stones—a Hawaiian altar. Attempting to warm your hands in your pockets, you recall that people once came here protected only by bark shawls. The guide sets up a portable telescope as the setting sun blazes its way through the thin, clear atmosphere. In the profound darkness left in its wake, you gaze on Saturn, then a nebula, then remnants of a supernova. When the glass is turned on the full moon, its brightness burns your eye. You blink, you tear, but you can't pull away.

IF YOU'VE EVER WANTED TO COME FACE TO FACE WITH ELEMENTAL creation and destruction, the Big Island is the place to do it. From Crater Rim Drive in Hawai'i Volcanoes National Park, look down into the rumpled, shining black pit that is the central crater of Kīlauea, the world's most continuously active volcano. The caldera is stiff and quiet today, but a sign tells you that as recently as 1974 it was a surging lake of molten rock. Turning onto Chain of Craters Road, you wind down the mountainside through the fantastic domain of Pele, goddess of volcanic fire. Evidences of chaotic natural forces meet you at every viewpoint—sharp-rimmed craters, dome-shaped cinder hills, and miles of gleaming, ropy black lava piled against the roadway. A few miles on, the road ends

The Hot Stuff

HAWAI'I VOLCANOES NATIONAL PARK, HAWAI'I

When lava moves, it glows like liquid sunshine. In a sense, that's what it is— the Earth spreading its molten inner light.

where lava has buried it under what look like massive globs of spilled pudding. You start to hike over the rolling wasteland toward the ocean. The expanse of stone has buckled and snapped like a hard cookie. Here and there you spot a rare glimmer of green: a fern sprouting from a hostile crevice. Two hours later you reach the collision point of new lava and cold sea. The heat from the ground soaks through your soles and pushes against your face. As you walk across the fresh crust, the surface shatters into black needles and you hear a glassy tinkling. Stepping across cracks, you stare down at the laser-bright orange of 2,000°F planet plasma. A wave smashes into the new black-sand beach. As it pulls back, steam bursts into the sky and salt frosts the cliffs. An enormous rock on a nearby ridge suddenly swells. Brilliant lava oozes from every seam, and again you hear that tinkling music.

EXTREME DANGER
BEYOND
THIS POINT!

With 500,000 cubic yards of new land
being created by lava flows each day, the
landscape looks a bit like a botched parking
lot. All this natural asphalt is just one
of the planet's marvels encountered here.

Writing in 1866 of his visit
to Kīlauea, Mark Twain wrote:
"I have seen Vesuvius since,
but it was a mere toy, a
child's volcano, a soup-kettle,
compared to this.... Here
was a yawning pit upon
whose floor the armies of
Russia could camp, and
have room to spare."

A GANG OF TATTOOED MEN IN LOINCLOTHS DESCENDS ON Lahaina's Front Street. Suddenly they stop, crouch, shake their spears, and shout belligerently at the crowd. The air fills with a hooting fanfare of conch shells—the start of a parade that could happen only in Polynesia. Behind these enthusiastic re-creations of warriors past, you glimpse the real stars of the day: the canoes. As they approach like mini Rose Bowl floats, each accompanied by a throng of foliage-clad dancers and musicians, you recognize a few you watched being built just this afternoon while you lounged in the warm shade of the town's giant banyan tree. From Tahiti and the Cook Islands, from New Zealand and Tonga and all over Hawai'i, master carvers came to create these distinctive canoes—sleek as skis—in only two weeks, whittling hulls from tree trunks

The Pride of the Race

IN CELEBRATION OF CANOES, LAHAINA, MAUI

Polynesians were crisscrossing the Pacific in their voyaging canoes at least a thousand years before Columbus learned to reef a sail.

at least 18 feet long. Chisel bites are still visible around the rough-cut rosettes along the gunwales. The parade ends at sunset at Lahaina Harbor, where chanting and drumbeats welcome the arrival of large voyaging canoes. The technological innovation of these two-hulled craft with curved crab-claw sails enabled Polynesians to do the impossible: navigate the vast Pacific without instruments. Today's celebration marks the midpoint of a two-week festival dedicated to these emblems of renewed traditions, of Polynesian solidarity, and of Hawaiians' pride in their heritage. Seeing the voyaging canoes in their primitive elegance, you can almost imagine those earlier Polynesians who swarmed like Vikings across thousands of miles of open ocean to settle these islands. A Hawaiian band launches into a set. Underneath the music you can hear the roar of the surf, beckoning men as ever to go down to the sea in ships...or canoes.

Canoe clubs preserve this slice of Hawaiian tradition. They also remind us that, long before Hawai'i became the 50th U.S. state, it was a leading member in the family of Polynesian island cultures.

WHEN IT COMES TO EXPLORING ARCHAEOLOGICAL RUINS, THE MORE REMOTE THE site, the better: the less of the present there is to intrude, the easier it is to reconstruct the pieces of a vanished world. So of all the mysterious remains of ancient settlements scattered across the islands, you've set your sights on Kaunolū, on the southwest coast of Lāna'i. Though it's only about 9 miles away as the crow flies, the drive from Mānele Bay takes an hour. Your jeep bumps along the rough roads; toward the end, the tires are fighting for every inch of ground. Finally you reach a plateau that juts out into the sea, fortified by stark cliffs more than 60 feet high. Dominating the site is a large *heiau,* a temple platform built of closely fitted stones. Called Halulu, it served as a place of refuge for those fleeing the brutal punishments of ancient law; Hawaiians still consider it sacred ground. You scrutinize the rocks and spot faint etchings here and

Written in Stone

KAUNOLŪ, LĀNA'I

Some heiaus, like Kaunolū's, provided refuge, while others were stages for human sacrifice. King Kamehameha had one built in 1790 and dedicated it with the blood of his chief rival.

there. One petroglyph found only at Kaunolū depicts a birdman, arms spread wide like wings. Stepping carefully, as if the images were chalk drawings your feet might erase, you make your way to Kahekili's Leap, a natural diving platform named for a Maui king who would prove his mettle by hurling himself off the cliff. It was a reckless trick, you decide—you can see coral-covered rocks just beneath the water's surface. But fishermen, not kings, built this village untold generations ago. You walk the old footpaths, passing canoe shelters, shrines, and remnants of house foundations— faded memories in stacked stone. To restore thatched roofs and laughing voices to this silent, lonely place requires another kind of bold leap: one of the imagination.

The whirlwind arrival of the Western world blew places like Kaunolū clean of inhabitants, leaving only stone upon stone: the foundations of houses, shrines to the gods of fishing, and the large platforms called heiaus, where the rituals and teachings of the ancient world were perpetuated.

Revered Outcasts

DAMIEN TOURS, KALAUPAPA, MOLOKA'I

LEATHER SQUEAKS, HOOFS CLAP ON STONE, AND THE SURF ROARS FAR BELOW. FROM ASTRIDE A mule you see the tiny Kalaupapa Peninsula sticking like the toe of a boot into the curling sea. You're riding a zigzag trail down the highest sea cliffs in the world, and though the mules are as solid and safe as sofas, remember the trick: don't look down. Once you reach the bottom, you're picked up by a dilapidated school bus. At the wheel is your guide, Richard Marks, Kalaupapa's sheriff. At first you wonder why he's moonlighting, but he explains that the only crime he has to deal with is reckless driving. "All our drivers here are half blind," says Marks, "but what can you do?" Kalaupapa has fewer than 50 residents, all of them over 60 and all victims of Hansen's disease, or leprosy, before the cure was developed. The last of a colony of exiles once numbering 2,000, they have chosen to finish their days together in this isolated place, respected for what they and the others endured. Marks stops at the

Lepers were once flung from boats and forced to swim here, to live and die alone, away from a world that feared them. Father Damien came to help—and died of the disease.

cemetery, and a woman gets out to look among the markers for her family name. She doesn't succeed. "It's usually that way," says the sheriff—lepers were encouraged to change their names and sever their family ties. The bus bounces across the peninsula as Marks tells the history of Kalaupapa—in his version, a string of colossal bureaucratic blunders, which he relates with the timing of a stand-up comedian. The passengers roar with laughter as he pulls up to St. Philomena Church, built by Father Damien in 1883. Inside the sanctuary Marks describes Damien's bullheaded struggles to help his banished congregation. At the time the priest was nearly excommunicated by Church authorities; today he's a candidate for sainthood.

IN THE MURMURS THAT POUR FROM UNDER THE TARP ROOFS OF THE HILO FARMERS Market you hear the sounds of polyglot Hawai'i: English is spoken here with every conceivable accent, from Thai and Tagalog to German. "How much you sell 'em?" says a voice. "One dollah." "I like have one." Your first sight is all floral—billowing masses of fresh-cut flowers. A dozen kinds of anthuriums wave like flags. As if the usual stop-sign-red ones aren't strange enough, here are big creamy-green ones, little snappy whites, even a lurid purple specimen that's cupped like a tulip. Mixed among them are buckets of sweet-smelling tuberoses, long-stemmed orchids, and crowds of calla lilies. The hubbub of voices draws you under a canopy where tropical produce is hawked by vendors of every description—barefoot Tongans, wizened farmers, bearded homesteaders. Instead of familiar apples, spuds, or asparagus, you find mangoes,

Common Wealth

FARMERS MARKET, HILO, HAWAI'I

In the 1920s Hilo was the commercial and architectural rival to Honolulu. Today it's still rich in history and, on market days, in the fruits of the land and sea.

taro, crunchy fern fronds, and rambutans in shaggy red jackets. Two-foot-long spears of bamboo shoots are lashed together like bundles of irrigation pipe. The farmers have driven here from every part of the Big Island, bringing breadfruit from the volcanic south, apple bananas from the windward coast, and rainbow papayas from Kapoho in the east. You pick up more sweet scents: banana *loompia* in its fried wrapper, the chewy Philippine doughnut called *cascaron,* red-bean buns. You puzzle over the prepared snacks, then opt for a confection in the raw: an old man uses a machete to split open a "spoon meat" coconut, and you scoop out the immature whiteness, soft as pudding. As you slurp up the cream, he tries to interest you in the head of an ahi fish or a bag of Poi Pounda poi. "Now," he says, "you eating like a Hawaiian."

HAOLE POKA
SWEET GRENADILLA

On islands surrounded by thousands of miles of ocean, a market spilling over with foods fresh from the fields is a potent symbol of the self-reliance and health of the community.

CURLING YOUR TOES INTO THE SAND, YOU LOOK ACROSS Waikīkī's long, impeccably white beach—hard to believe that 100 years ago it was a swamp. Ahead is the Diamond Head peak, its shape familiar from all those pineapple ads. You're standing next to the bronze statue of Duke Kahanamoku, the consummate Waikīkī beach boy, whose aloha spirit and surfing and swimming prowess made this beach—barged over grain by grain from Moloka'i—the most famous in the world. Behind him, as if planted upright in the sand, is his longboard. You need no further prompting—surf's up! Soon you're on a surfboard of your own, paddling out into the clear turquoise sea, passing boogie-boarders and old folks bobbing in the warm water. A sleek red outrigger canoe with five paddlers races past you. This is the easiest place in the world to learn to surf, said the

The Beach of All Beaches

WAIKĪKĪ, HONOLULU, O'AHU

The beach that started beach culture in the days of bloomers, not string bikinis, this is the Hawai'i of everyone's imagination.

beach boy who rented you the board. And with a board this big, he said, you can't fall: it's like standing on the sidewalk. Of course you fall a few times anyway, but soon you get the hang of it. When you finally get your balance and start racing toward shore, you look up to see the huge beach dotted with sunbathers and, behind them, the glittering high-rises of Waikīkī's golden mile. Later you walk the spangly main boulevard, Kalākaua Avenue, the beach's counter-reality. You weave down sidewalks crowded with sunburnt honeymooners, Japanese women carrying bags from Chanel and Celine, street performers, and thousands doing exactly what you're doing: enjoying the carnival. The bright jangle of ukuleles from a beachside bar draws you in for a drink and a ringside seat for the daily sunset show. As the beach turns amber and rose, you decide to wait right here for moonrise.

Sixty-five thousand people a day make their way to the ongoing carnival that is Waikīkī. Before them, so did Charlie Chaplin and Babe Ruth, Jack London and Robert Louis Stevenson, Gidget and Moondoggie.

MOST PEOPLE ARE CONTENT TO EXPLORE THE LOWER POOLS OF Maui's 'Ohe'o Gulch—but *you* know the gulch is only the starting point for a walk to reach the real prize, an easy 2 miles away. Leaving behind the sunbathers draped over the rocks, you set your sights on Waimoku Falls, a 400-foot cascade hidden in the hills. The first mile of the trail climbs steadily uphill, in the shade of guava and mango trees, following the crashing noise of Palikea Stream. It tumbles from pool to pool, each basin a curve of basalt hollowed out by the churning water. Side trails to a swimming hole or a lesser waterfall tempt you—yield or forge ahead. Midway the trail changes. You cross a dizzying ravine by footbridge, then lose yourself in a forest of bamboo. There's nothing quite like a bamboo forest for giving you the feeling that you've been swallowed.

The Majesty of Water

WAIMOKU FALLS, KĪPAHULU, MAUI

Waterfalls, each with its own personality, inhabit every one of Hawai'i's steep, stream-sliced canyons. You could spend a lifetime trying to visit them all.

Inside, the light dims and you're surrounded by a serene monotony of slick green poles. In the still, heavy air the sound of your voice wanders and disappears. When the wind gusts, you don't feel it, but you hear it rattling the slender leaves high overhead. A moment later the whole forest starts swaying, the hollow trunks clonking together like a tuneless marimba band. Breaking out at last, you continue to climb, picking your way across rocky brooks. Finally you turn the corner and enter Waimoku's presence. She usually appears lacy and meek, though the force of the water sends wet blasts of wind against your face. When rain strikes the mountain above, she'll suddenly explode. People have been known to turn and run.

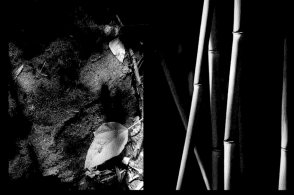

Enter the lush tropical rain forest. Walk on paths edged with ferns and flowers past trees offering up their fruits. Dipping under trailing vines, press on through the tall bamboos until you come to Waimoku. In awe, you'll tip your head way back to follow the soft, feathery spill of the water, but don't be fooled: seemingly so light, it is strong enough to knock you down.

THE RUSTY SPRING SQUEAKS AS THE WOODEN SCREEN DOOR BANGS SHUT BEHIND you. The air is thick with the steam of boiling noodles. A sign over the kitchen window says: "No checks accepted. Please do not stick gum under counter thank you." You pull up a stool and sit down. Hamura Saimin Shop has only one counter, and it winds through the room like a...well, like a noodle. No need to dawdle over a menu, because there's only one choice: the Japanese meal-in-a-bowl soup called *saimin*. Hamura's take on the working-class dish—a classic example of a homegrown style of culture-bending cuisine known simply as local food—keeps the stools filled every day, and has been doing so for 50 years. A thousand bowls a day. The woman in the kitchen window presides over a confusion of kettles in which noodles and broth bubble away as her hands dart between bowls of chopped ham, broccoli, hard-boiled egg, roast pork, fish

Original Fast Food

HAMURA SAIMIN SHOP, LĪHUʻE, KAUAʻI

"Local food" evolved out of sugar plantation workers' camps, where appetites were hearty, time and money scarce, and ethnicities chop suey—all mixed up.

cake, green onion, and wontons. You order the "Special," which comes with everything, then take a pair of cheap chopsticks, snap them apart, and scrape them together to rub off the splinters. From the bottles and jars on the counter you choose mustard and soy sauce, mixing them to make a dipping sauce, and turn a wary eye toward the shaker of vinegar-water with whole Hawaiian chilies at the bottom, loosing their fire into the liquid. Your bowl arrives, and you stab your chopsticks into the steaming noodles. Lift and slurp, pick and dip—once you start, it's too good to stop. Finally, you spoon up the remaining broth, and it's on to dessert. Of course there's only one, and it's perfect: passionfruit chiffon pie.

IT'S AN ODD RITUAL ON MAUI—GET UP AT THREE IN THE MORNING and drive to the coldest place on the island, joining a line of people at the top of Haleakalā mountain. Everyone is wrapped in hotel blankets, shivering and hopping from foot to foot, waiting. As the sun touches the horizon and spreads golden fire across the clouds, it lights up other volcanoes that have pushed their way out of the sea: the two great peaks of the Big Island, Mauna Kea and Mauna Loa; the West Maui Mountains; and beyond them, Moloka'i. It also illuminates the marvelous sight in front of you: Haleakalā Crater. Once this steep-sided pit was a lake big enough to float the island of Manhattan in. You can see the two gaps, like cracks in a bowl, where the water drained away. You stow your blankets and hike

Doing the Crater

SUMMIT, HALEAKALĀ NATIONAL PARK, MAUI

At the "House of the Sun," higher than airplanes and clouds, the dawn unveils a great chasm—an unearthly world left behind as testimony to infernal forces.

down Sliding Sands Trail, slushing and crunching on slopes streaked with the rusty reds, ochers, and blacks of ancient lava and ash flows. On the crater floor you trek for miles between cinder cones up to 600 feet high. Dotting the flanks of these hills of rubble spewed by minivolcanoes are what look like big silver balloons. As you get closer you see that they're silverswords, plants found nowhere else, which bloom spectacularly once in 20 years and then die. There are more weird sights on another looping path: the Bottomless Pit and Pele's Paint Pot, a stretch of trail that passes through a landscape spattered with cinders in every color on the fire goddess's palette. Late in the afternoon you head out up a steep switchback. It's a tough hike, especially the last mile. But once you're back on the rim, you take a last look into the crater and have to fight the urge to go right back down again.

Weather appears and
disappears before your eyes.
Rain falls sideways, or even
upward. Afternoon clouds
surge up Koʻolau Gap,
blanketing the peak called
"mist maker." Some years
it snows, and you see cars
at the beach with snowmen
mounted on their bumpers.

PASSING THROUGH A GAP IN A LOW FIELDSTONE WALL, YOU ENTER THE deep shade of macadamias and short rows of coffee trees. The farmer takes a break from hoeing carrots to "talk story" for a bit. The beetles are chewing up his string beans, he says, but last year he harvested 50 bags of coffee cherries. Built early last century by one of many Japanese immigrant families who ended up growing coffee in Kona, this is still a working farm, though one frozen in time. The interpreters are living the lives of their grandparents, with an earlier era's tools and grace. At the farmhouse, your kimono-clad hostess politely requests that you leave your shoes at the door. (Only a barbarian would tromp dirt through these pristine, plain rooms.) You follow her in, past faded pictures of a Japanese emperor and his wife that adorn walls of raw Douglas fir. At a small Buddhist

The Coffee Life

KONA COFFEE LIVING HISTORY MUSEUM, KEALAKEKUA, HAWAI‘I

Walk (shoeless) in the footsteps of the Uchidas, who for 80 years lived lives of quiet dignity here, preserving their traditions far from their homeland.

shrine she lights a candle and rings a bell. Another woman, working at a treadle-operated sewing machine, stops to show you hats and raincoats she's made from cotton rice sacks. In the kitchen your hostess offers a snack of farm greens dressed in soy sauce, vinegar, and mustard. Blowing on embers through a length of bamboo, she fires up the twig-fueled stove, cooks some rice, then shows you how to form it into *musubi,* the seaweed-wrapped staple of a farmer's lunch. As a girl, she says, she was told to "make nice triangles and get a handsome husband." Back outside, you're taken to see how the pulp is removed from the coffee cherries using a Rube Goldbergesque mill, and how the beans (the seeds) are dried on a high platform, protected by an ingenious rollaway roof. Only the sound of a donkey braying hungrily disturbs the tractorless silence.

From earth swept with a handmade rake
to a faded photograph on a shelf—a couple
posing stiffly in their holiday finery—life
on the farm remains much as it ever was.
At any moment the pioneer family could
return and pick up where they left off.

IT'S A COOL MORNING IN THE SUNNY SOUTH OF THE GARDEN ISLE, and you're riding along the edge of a sharp-sided jungle valley. A curving lagoon marks your first stop, one of two National Botanical Garden sites you can visit in a day—a pair of Edens. On the raked paths of Allerton Garden you walk in deep shade as unseen birds chatter overhead. Through a parting in the trees you come upon the first "room": the Diana Pool, mirroring a temple folly and a statue of the goddess of the hunt. In the next room, the Mermaid Fountain, a sheet of water pulsates between ribbons of concrete. Allerton is a masterpiece of landscape design, its carefully composed scenes set in a valley so verdant it's hard to tell where design stops and nature begins. You continue to wander past prehistoric-looking fig trees whose pleated roots embraced

Kingdom of Leaves

NATIONAL TROPICAL BOTANICAL GARDEN, KAUA'I

The ancient Hawaiian word for fresh water *(wai)* was also the word for wealth *(waiwai)*. From that perspective, the inhabitants of Kaua'i's deep, well-watered valleys were prosperous indeed.

some recent cinematic dinosaur eggs, then sit by a bronze Buddha and listen to the music of a stream. At Limahuli Garden, halfway around the island near the start of the Nā Pali Coast, the emphasis is reversed: instead of tailoring nature, this garden works to restore it. Here the invasive jungle is being pushed back from an entire valley to make room for endangered native flora. The a'lula, for example, once called "a cabbage on a baseball bat," had dwindled to fewer than 100 specimens clinging to the nearby cliffs, but now the bats are swinging again. Where Allerton's gardens are luxuriant, Limahuli's landscape is young, its plants still establishing themselves. In the late-afternoon sun you gaze up at a volcanic spire at the head of the valley, then over the restored taro ponds that stair-step from the valley floor. Your mind is quiet, saturated with green.

Intoxicated by the abundant sunlight and water, plants from around the world have taken to these valleys with enthusiasm, squeezing out thousands of species that live only here. The National Tropical Botanical Garden is working to turn the tide.

NEXT TIME YOU HAVE A CRAVING FOR SEA CUCUMBERS, HEAD TO one of the shops on the corner of Honolulu's Mauna Kea and Hotel streets. While you're there, pick up some fungus (it looks like a yellow kitchen sponge), some *look funn* noodles, and a few of those 1,000-year-old duck eggs with the red yolks. As you thread your way along the narrow sidewalks of Chinatown you're plunged into a pan-Asian environment, but one whose Hawaiian character keeps surfacing. For example, this is the best place to buy a lei, one of those flower garlands worn when you're arriving, departing, graduating, having a birthday, feeling good, or simply wanting to feel good. It's hard to be glum with gardenias, roses, or orchids around your neck. At the M.P. Lei Shop, elders sit at cramped tables, carefully sculpting leis from Maunaloa orchids. You choose a gleaming

Dried Sea Cucumbers & Leis

CHINATOWN, HONOLULU, O'AHU

Yes, Hawai'i this is. Should confusion set in as you're wandering among purveyors of everything Oriental, pop into a lei shop and back to Honolulu.

white necklace of tuberoses, pay the ridiculous price—just a few bucks—and settle its cool, fragrant weight on your shoulders. With your lei as a reality check, you plunge into the hubbub of the food court. Here, in the dim light, people crowd the tile tables, gossiping in a half-dozen languages, smoking cigarettes, and wolfing down Philippine *pancit* (noodles and pork), Malaysian *nasi goreng* (spicy fried rice), or Korean *mandoo* (dumpling soup). Around the corner the proprietor of the Ying Leong Look Funn Factory offers you samples of his fat, evanescent noodles and teaches you how to say "it's good" in his Chinese dialect. He smiles. So does the woman at the Laotian market who hands you an unrecognizable fruit and says, "Try. You eat when it get soft." It's not just the lei shops that make Chinatown Hawaiian. It's this welcoming warmth known as the aloha spirit.

THE VIEWPOINT OVERLOOKING THE HANALEI VALLEY OFFERS ONE of Hawai'i's most gladdening sights: a landscape of shining ponds, some silvery blue, mirroring the sky, others bright green with gently waving leaves. Today, instead of driving past them, you turn off the main road and stop at Haraguchi Farms. Standing amid his 30 acres of fields, called *lo'i*, is Rod Haraguchi. Like his neighbors, Rod's on a mission to bring back taro, once the mainstay of Hawaiian culture, and he welcomes the chance to tell you a thing or two about it. "The mud is good for you," he begins, explaining why he works barefoot. Some of his farmhands, wading through one lo'i, are harvesting, yanking the plants out roots and all. A flick of a machete strips off the leaves. Another flick isolates the potatolike corm, which will end up pounded into a suspicious-looking, bland-

The Good Mud

TARO FIELDS, HANALEI, KAUA'I

Taro sustained Hawaiian culture in the way buffalo sustained the Plains Indians. Today, more than 60 percent of the crop grows in Hanalei.

tasting gray paste called poi. The midstems are set aside for replanting. In a nearby lo'i workers are doing just that, stirring the waters mud-red as they plunge the slender cuttings into the flooded earth. Taro is an excellent food, Rod says, since it's nonallergenic and high in calcium; the greens, he claims, Popeye would have loved. He takes you to see the old rice mill his great-grandfather used back when local farmers worked paddies, not lo'i. The diesel-driven contraption fills several rooms. It stayed in service until the 1960s, when area farmers decided to return to *kalo,* as Hawaiians call the starchy crop that had been grown here since prehistoric times. Leaving the fields behind, you stop at the farm's roadside stand. Its Kalo Kooler, loaded with fresh tropical fruit, beats any milk-based smoothie hands down. One slurp and you believe: what grows in this good mud is the original perfect food.

"HAI-YAW! HAI-YAW!" SHOUTS A MAN ON HORSEBACK ABOVE THE muffled thunder of hooves. Serious-faced calves crowd into the weighing pen, and the gate clangs shut. Another swings open, and hooves thunder again. "Weet-hah!" The sounds of Hawai'i? You bet. This is 'Ulupalakua Ranch, on Haleakalā's leeward slopes—a 23,000-acre spread that maintains the 170-year-old traditions of the *paniolo*, or cowboy. It's one of only a handful of large ranches still operating in Hawai'i, and today you're in luck: the cowboys are working the pens along the roadside. You watch for a while, listening to the paniolos' bursts of pidgin English, but since punching cattle takes as much concentration as juggling chain saws, you save your questions for the tour.

Tropical Cowboys

'ULUPALAKUA RANCH, 'ULUPALAKUA, MAUI

The islands' first cattle and horses were imported, as were the vaqueros who taught Hawaiians to rope and ride in the 1830s. By the early 1900s ranching dominated the islands.

"Hope you don't mind, but we're going to get a little dirty," says the driver as the jeep climbs the steeply tilted landscape heaped with cinder cones and streaked black with crumbling lava flows. Dust flying everywhere, you pass a few cows, then spot a herd of elk in the distance. Near the top of the ranch you get out to explore an enormous cave, actually a lava tube left behind when a red-hot river drained away. The ranch is honeycombed with such tubes, one of the paniolos' job hazards. After the tour, you dust off and visit the small museum. One corner is dedicated to Cowboy Hall of Famer Ikua Purdy, foreman here for most of his life. (The men you saw weighing calves are his grandsons.) In 1908 Purdy showed up in Wyoming for the world steer-roping championship. With a few deft moves, he turned the crowd's snickers into cheers. It shouldn't have been such a surprise that he walked away with the title—after all, Hawaiian cowboys had been at it a lot longer.

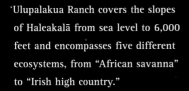

'Ulupalakua Ranch covers the slopes of Haleakalā from sea level to 6,000 feet and encompasses five different ecosystems, from "African savanna" to "Irish high country."

Born Again

KA HULA PIKO FESTIVAL, KALUAKO'I, MOLOKA'I

IT'S AN HOUR BEFORE DAWN, AND HUNDREDS OF PEOPLE SIT SILENTLY ON A BARE MOLOKA'I hilltop that myth proclaims the birthplace of hula. Suddenly from the darkness comes a sonorous blast of conch shells. A man's voice starts to chant—powerful, furious, shaking the stars. You hear the rustle of people rising around you, and now the first dances commence. On this solemn note begins a day that will be anything but. The *ho'olaule'a*—celebration day—of the weeklong Ka Hula Piko Festival is the best open-air, no-ticket-needed party in Hawai'i. Once it's fully light, you give yourself a muscle-loosening shake and head down the hill to the beach park, where musicians are setting up in the bandstand. Booths surrounding a grassy field entice you with pickled mango and lū'au stew, custom-built ukuleles, and hand-printed pareus. You find a choice spot just before the first *hālau* (hula school)—one of dozens that have come from every island to this remote place—

From here, legend says a woman/goddess named Laka traveled throughout the islands teaching the dance that is today the emblem of Hawaiian culture.

begins its dance. Despite the precision and fervent drama of the performances, the spirit of the day is noncompetitive and hang-loose. Decked in leaves and flowers, the dancers perform barefoot. The men grunt and stomp the earth, driven by the insistent rhythms pounded out on huge drums. The women's arms slide upward with the high, trembling harmonies of the singers, hands gathering up the breezes the song celebrates. Between events, emcees satirize everyone from the governor to audience members, and the bands rock the park with Hawaiian music. Gourds rattle, hips swish, and the crowd slowly shifts into the shade. You adjourn to your blanket, warmed by the energy of the sun and the dance.

LĀNA'I IS SHAPED LIKE A TIPPED SAUCER, ONE RIM DUNKING into the sea, the other arcing into the sky. As you drive out of Lāna'i City you see the crest, with a dirt track running along it. You turn your jeep off the paved road and shift into four-wheel drive—you've been itching to since you arrived. You speed along on flat ground until you catch the heel of the ridge and start to climb. In the dry forest, ironwood needles blanket the red earth. Posted signs tell you this is hunting country, the terrain of pheasants, deer, and mouflon sheep. Then the road turns and you begin riding the ridge. The land falls away sharply on either side. To windward are the blue sea channel and five islands, their jagged summits snagged by clouds. To leeward is Lāna'i's soft, reassuring landscape. The curves of the land taper off into the distance, silvery, hazy light blurring

Riding the Rim

THE MUNRO TRAIL, LĀNA'IHALE, LĀNA'I

their contours. Hikers scramble up the bank to let you by—the road is just wide enough for a car. After you pass the summit marker and start the gradual descent, you see something you scarcely would expect on this arid island: mist. The road gets muddy; the mist rises over your head. The branches of the tall pines literally comb water out of the air. Drops of it splat onto the windshield and patter on the metal of your jeep. Finally the road dries out for a shady, forested finish as it loops back to Lāna'i City. There you debark, as if from your seat on a roller-coaster.

The sharp peaks of Maui and Moloka'i bite into the blue horizon. From Lāna'i's summit ridge, they show themselves for what they are: audacious, hard-boned cloud catchers.

The Munro Trail is named for New Zealand naturalist George Munro, who planted this ridge with Cook and Norfolk Island pines in the 1930s. The thin trees' brushy branches collect moisture from the fog—each tree drips about 33 gallons of cool sky juice a day.

THERE ARE FEW PLACES LEFT ON EARTH WHERE ONLY YOUR FEET CAN TAKE YOU. Not even a small horse would fit on some stretches of the 11-mile trail to the Kalalau Valley, on Kauaʻi's Nā Pali Coast. *Pali* means "cliff," and in these places the path is scarcely wider than your boot, a mere scratch along a vertical wall hundreds of feet high. For the first 2 miles, though, starting at Kēʻē Beach, the going is fairly easy. The ample path winds in and out of slim, forested valleys. The ocean glimmers below. On the clear blue expanse you spot a sailboat that looks no bigger than a bathtub toy or a kayak the size of an apostrophe. Rounding a bend, you descend into a deep, bright valley called Hanakāpīʻai. Other hikers are there already, soaking their feet in the stream, picking their way down to the beach, or looking for the overgrown trail that leads up to a waterfall. You're tempted, but you push on. Next come the challenges of

The Heart of Lightness

KALALAU TRAIL, NĀ PALI COAST, KAUAʻI

Hikers rank this trek—11 grueling, thrilling miles through the primeval landscape of Spielberg's Jurassic Park—alongside Nepal and Machu Picchu.

the cliff walk, and for 4 miles there isn't even room for your thoughts. Finally you reach the next big stream, at Hanakoa Valley. In this deeply shaded wilderness, dragonflies dart over tumbled stones, the remnants of an ancient settlement. Now you *need* a break—and plunge your feet into the stream. It's 5 more aerial miles to the trail's end, at the mouth of the valley. There a huge, empty white beach glows with heat in the afternoon sun. A tall waterfall strikes the rocks behind it—a natural shower. You shed your clothes, lean back against the cliff, and let the cold water bang on your head. Here, surrounded by Nā Pali's brute magnificence, civilization is very far away.

Simple stuff. That's what you get to. Yellow leaf bobbing in a green pool. Shining blue sea dabbled with cloud shadows. Timeless boulders. And reality, the world stripped to its essentials. You could hold it in your hands if only your hands weren't human.

The ancient Hawaiians thrived in Nā Pali's deep cathedral valleys, on which civilization has not encroached. Long passed from human memory, they now belong to the birds, the trees, and the unrestrained fertility of sunlight.

All the Details

The state of Hawai'i is made up of eight major and 114 minor volcanic and coral islands scattered about the Pacific Ocean. Major carriers flying into Honolulu (O'ahu), the main airport, include American (tel. 800/433-7300), Continental (tel. 800/525-0280), Delta (tel. 800/221-1212), and United (tel. 800/241-6522); some also serve Maui, Kaua'i, and the Big Island. In addition, two homegrown carriers—Aloha Airlines (tel. 800/367-5250, www.alohaair.com) and Hawaiian Airlines (tel. 800/367-5320, www.hawaiianair.com)—offer flights from the mainland (about five hours), as well as interisland hops (20 to 30 minutes each). Aloha, with 170 interisland flights a day, offers direct service to Honolulu and Maui from Oakland, California. Hawaiian flies direct to Honolulu from Los Angeles, San Francisco, Las Vegas, Seattle, and Portland, Oregon, and to Maui from L.A.

You can see the islands by taking a taxi from the plane to your hotel, then signing up for guided tours. Otherwise, you'll want to rent a car. Aside from the Honolulu city bus system—which is efficient, cheap, and crowded—public transportation scarcely exists here. Amazingly, the only interisland ferry is the 45-minute shuttle that plies between Lahaina on Maui and Mānele Bay on Lāna'i five times a day.

There is little seasonal change on the islands, either in room rates (10%–15% higher mid-December to mid-April) or in weather. Almost 1,500 miles north of the equator, they are tropical without being steamy, cooled by trade winds. Expect mostly blue skies and balmy days: afternoon temperatures in resort areas near sea level average 75°F in the coldest months, December and January, and may reach 92°F in August and September. The mercury does drop quickly when you drive up into the mountains. For more information, contact the Hawai'i Visitors and Convention Bureau (2270 Kalākaua Ave., Suite 801, Honolulu, HI 96817, tel. 808/923-1811, www.gohawaii.com).

Note: *Unless otherwise stated, listed lodgings are open year-round, accept credit cards, and have rooms with private baths. Grid coordinates, given in parentheses after town names, refer to the maps on pages 80–82.*

HAWAI'I

"The Big Island" is about twice the size of all the others put together, and still growing—lava has been flowing since January 1983. There are two airports, two hours apart: one's in Hilo, on the windward side, and the other,

Keāhole airport, is on the barren lava flats of the leeward, or *kona*, side. The main town on the Kona side is Kailua-Kona. This is the best of the islands for driving: the highways are straight, well-paved, and without traffic. It hasn't developed much and hasn't really caught on with tourists—which makes it all the more pleasant to explore. You can hike into volcanic craters, fish for marlin, explore cowboy country, or sunbathe on beaches of black lava, white coral, or green olivine. For more information, contact the Big Island Visitors Bureau (250 Keawe St., Hilo, HI 96720, tel. 808/961–5797 or 800/648–2441, www.bigisland.org).

EAST RIFT ZONE, HAWAI'I VOLCANOES NATIONAL PARK (14I)
The Hot Stuff, p. 16

The park encompasses a quarter-million acres, including the summit of Mauna Loa. From the end of 20-mile Chain of Craters Road, off the 11-mile ring road that circles the sleeping Kīlauea Caldera, it's possible to walk to where the lava's flowing (though not likely fountaining—this volcano doesn't shoot into the air much). Two disclaimers: First, no one can predict where the flow will occur on a given day. Second, people have died while behaving stupidly around hot lava. By the time you begin your hike, park rangers at both the visitor center and the end of Chain of Craters Road will have tried to teach you everything you need to know so you don't behave stupidly.

CONTACT: Hawai'i Volcanoes National Park, Box 52, Hawai'i National Park, HI 96718-0052, tel. 808/985-6000, www.nps.gov/havo.

DISTANCES: 30 mi south of Hilo, 95 mi southeast of Kailua.

PRICES: Admission $10.

LODGING: In the village just outside the park entrance and visitor center are the handsome, antiques-filled **Hale Ohi'a Cottages.** Set amid charming gardens in which forest birds trill, this is a quiet, sensual place with romantic touches like fireplaces, a hot tub, and a splashing fountain. Box 758, Vol-

cano Village, HI 96785, tel. 808/967–7986 or 800/455–3803, fax 808/967–8610, www.haleohia.com. 3 cottages, 3 suites. $75–$130, with breakfast. Also in the village with views of the forest is the **Volcano Inn,** a wonderful B&B comprising a rambling house and cedar cottages trimmed with tree trunks and limbs. 19–3820 Old Volcano Hwy., Volcano Village, HI 96785, tel. 808/967–7293 or 800/997–2292, fax 808/985–7349, www.volcanoinn.com. 5 rooms, 4 cottages, with TV/VCRs, phone, cooking facilities, some fireplaces. $75–$130, with a big breakfast.

OPTIONS: A scenic chopper ride is a magnificent experience anywhere in Hawai'i, but especially here—you'll get to fly over the source vent, a hill from Hell called Pu'u 'O'o, and you'll get a video of your flight to take home. **Blue Hawaiian Helicopters** (tel. 808/871–8844, 808/961–5600, or 800/745–BLUE, www.bluehawaiian.com) is tops in efficiency, friendliness, safety, and quality of equipment.

FARMERS MARKET, HILO (16H)
Common Wealth, p. 32

The Hilo Farmers Market comes to life twice a week—every Wednesday and Saturday "from dawn 'til it's gone" (about 4 PM). To find it, look for the silver tarps that fill both sides of the street where Mamo Street meets Kamehameha Avenue, near the bay. When it's over, give yourself a walking tour of Hilo's well-preserved downtown with many historic buildings. A map is available at the tourist office (corner of Keawe and Haili Sts.), or get one when you visit Lyman Mission House and Museum (276 Haili St., tel. 808/935–5021), which deals with all aspects of Hilo's history, particularly its missionary days. Head 4 miles east of town for classic island-style cooking at the Seaside Restaurant (1790 Kalaniana'ole Ave., tel. 808/935–8825), in an old house overhanging beautiful ponds that yield the catch of the day.

CONTACT: Keith De La Cruz, Box 34, Hilo, HI 96721-0034, tel. 808/933–1000, Hilofarmersmrkt@aol.com.

LODGING: Jack London slept here; Queen Lili'uokalani, the last Hawaiian monarch, smoked cigars at the great dining room table. Your hostess at the **Shipman House**—you are literally a guest in her elegant, antiques-filled Victorian mansion—is a descendant of one of the first missionaries to Hawai'i. 131 Ka'iulani St., Hilo, HI 96720, tel./fax 808/934–8002 or tel. 800/627–8447, www.hilo-hawaii.com. 3 rooms, 2 cottage units, with minifridges. $150, with a grand breakfast. **Hawai'i Naniloa Resort,** with rooms overlooking the bay, sets the standard for efficiency and convenience. 93 Banyan Dr., Hilo, HI 96720, tel. 808/969–3333 or 800/367–5360, fax 808/969–6622, www.naniloa.com. 308 rooms, 17 suites, with A/C, TV. 2 restaurants, 2 pools, 9-hole golf course, health club, beauty salon. From $100.

OPTIONS: Other farmer's markets can be found in **Kailua** (12I) (Kona Inn parking lot, Ali'i Dr.; same days and times as Hilo event), in **Volcano Village** (15J) (Cooper Center; Sun. 8–10 AM), and in **Waimea** (13G) (Hawaiian Homes Hall; Sat. 7–10 AM). On **Maui,** in Kahului (9D), try the Wednesday market at the old Kahului Shopping Center (Ka'ahumanu Ave. between Pu'unene and Lono Aves.; 7 AM 'til noon or so) or the Maui Swap Meet (Pu'unene Ave., near Kamehameha Ave.; Wed. and Sat. from 8 AM). On **Kaua'i,** "sunshine markets" are held six days a week at 10 locations (check the visitors bureau for schedule). On **O'ahu** you'll find markets every day at one of 20 sites (call 808/522–7088).

KONA COFFEE LIVING HISTORY MUSEUM, KEALAKEKUA (12J)
The Coffee Life, p. 50

Kona coffee country occupies the most sheltered side of Mauna Loa. The huge mountain repels or absorbs the rest of the world, leaving this patch of steep terrain with weather and an attitude all its own. Afternoon clouds and showers ease the intensity of the sun here, and the soil is deep and porous. Conditions are perfect for growing coffee. This is a region of independents, farmers and ranchers of all races who resisted the plantation mentality and made a life of their own. Their stories and the former Uchida Farm—worked by a Japanese family until 1991 yet never modernized—are preserved by the Kona Historical Society, which offers a wide range of activities, including walking tours of Kailua. The society's headquarters is itself a piece of local history: the

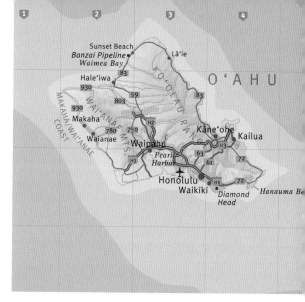

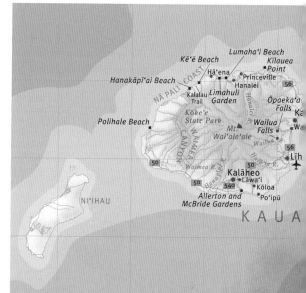

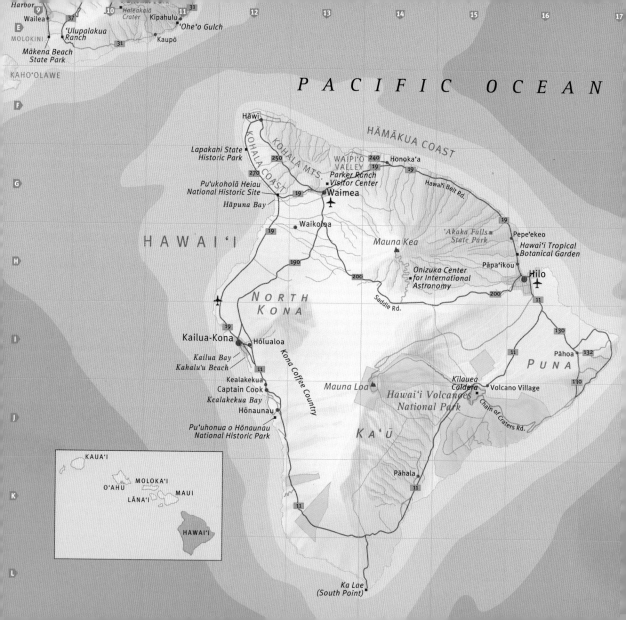

old rock-and-mortar Greenwell Store, on Hwy. 11 in Kalukalu, which served area farmers as far back as the 1870s.

CONTACT: Kona Historical Society, Box 398, Captain Cook, HI 96704, tel. 808/323–2006, www.konahistorical.org. The farm is at 81–6551 Māmalahoa Hwy., Kealakekua.

DISTANCES: 1¼ mi from Kealakekua, 10 mi south of Kailua.

PRICES: Admission $30 adults, $15 children.

LODGING: The best inn in coffee country, and one of the best in the state, is the **Hōlualoa Inn,** a rambling, luxurious cedar house with eucalyptus floors. The setting—on 40 acres of coffee and fruit trees—is lovely, with a grand view down the steep mountain to sunsets over the glittering bay. Breakfast, included, is lavish; sunsets come with gourmet cheeses and fresh island fruit. Box 222, Hōlualoa, HI 96725, tel. 800/392–1812 or 808/324–1121, fax 808/322–2472, www.konaweb.com/HINN. 4 rooms, 2 suites. Pool, hot tub in garden, billiard room. $150–$195.

OPTIONS: For something completely different, pop into the up-to-date **Greenwell Farms** (81–6581 Māmalahoa Hwy., Kealakekua, tel. 808/323–2862), where you can buy its coffee and macadamia nuts, sample various coffees, and tour the farm and mill. Moloka'i's **Coffees of Hawai'i** (Farrington Hwy. near Hwy. 470, Kualapu'u [7C], tel. 808/567–9241) offers mule-drawn wagon tours of its 500-acre plantation and coffee-processing plant weekdays at 10 and 1. At the state's largest coffee plantation, the **Kaua'i Coffee Company,** exhibits in the visitor center (Hwy. 540, between Kalāheo [4G] and 'Ele'ele, tel. 808/335–0813, www.kauaicoffee.com) show how the crop is grown and processed. In Maui, on the slopes of Haleakalā, stop at **Grandma's Coffee** (153 Kula Hwy., Kēōkea [9E], tel. 808/878–2140, www.grandmascoffee.com), a down-home eatery featuring brews made from organically grown East Maui beans; see the century-old roaster behind a window of the roasting room.

SUMMIT, MAUNA KEA (14H)
The Tallest Mountain on Earth, p. 14

The summit of Mauna Kea is the highest spot in the Hawaiian Islands. The name means "white mountain," no doubt for Mauna Kea's usual winter lid of snow—yes, people do ski and snowboard it, but there's no lift, and the trip to the top requires four-wheel drive. In a standard rental car you can drive to the 9,000-foot level and stop in at the Visitor Information Station (weekdays 9–noon, 1–5; weekends 9–6), with free displays that tell about the observatories. From 6 to 10 nightly, stargazers can get coffee and escape the cold in a shelter at the station.

CONTACT: Onizuka Center for International Astronomy, Visitor Information Station, tel. 808/961–2180, fax 808/969–4892, www.ifa.hawaii.edu/info/vis. Mauna Kea Observatories Support Services, 177 Maka'ala St., Hilo, HI 96720-5108, tel. 808/935–3371, fax 808/969–7673.

DISTANCES: 30 mi west of Hilo, 48 mi east of Kailua-Kona.

LODGING: There are no overnight accommodations near Mauna Kea. See other Big Island listings.

OPTIONS: If you're 16 or older and fit enough for the altitude, consider joining the station's free **summit tours** weekends from 1 to 5 PM; you'll need a four-wheel-drive vehicle, which you can rent in Hilo or Kailua. **Hawai'i Forest & Trail's** 8-hour tours (tel. 800/464–1993 or 808/331–8505, www.hawaii-forest.com) take you to the summit for sunset, then stop at the station for stargazing; the enthusiastic young company also offers trips to waterfalls, cloud forests, caves, and bird-watching sites.

HAWAI'I HIGHLIGHTS

If you're drawn to the romance of vanished Hawai'i, you can spend a full day driving north from the ancient temple compound at Pu'uhonua o Hōnaunau (12J) along the leeward coast, stopping at several such sites (see Options in "Written in Stone," p. 87), ending at the island's north tip in the haunting solitude of Mo'okini Heiau, an impressive place of worship built around AD 480 near the town of Hāwī (12F). This route also takes you past **Kealakekua Bay**, where Captain Cook was killed in a ruckus with the Hawaiians, now a marine preserve with great snorkeling; and past several **resort/golf** developments and some of the island's best beaches, especially **Hāpuna Bay** (12G). Also in the north, in the lovely, rolling Kohala Mountains, the modern-looking town of **Waimea** (13G) offers a taste of Hawaiian cowboy culture (see "Tropical Cowboys," p. 62). The city of **Hilo** (16H) is a historic artifact in its own right (see "Common Wealth," p. 32). From Hilo, spend a day driving north along the **Hāmākua Coast** just for the lush drama of the island's windward side. At **Ka Lae** (14L), stand in the driving wind facing the furious sea at the southernmost spot in the United States.

KAUAʻI

As soon as a volcanic island stops growing, it begins melting away under the influence of the rain. Kauaʻi, the oldest of the principal Hawaiian islands and thus the most "melted," demonstrates how lush and beautiful such erosion can be. Kauaʻi shows its age in unusual geographical features—monumental Waimea Canyon, for example, and several waterways big enough to merit the name "river" (something none of the other islands can boast). A huge, inaccessible swamp lies beneath Waiʻaleʻale, a mountain that is the rainiest spot on Earth. By the same geologic logic, this is a great island for beaches and flowers. For the most part, Kauaians live around the edges of the island in small villages linked by a belt road that circles about three-fourths of Kauaʻi, dead-ending when it reaches the fierce Nā Pali Coast. The main town, and site of the airport, is Līhuʻe. For more information, contact the Kauaʻi Visitors Bureau (4334 Rice St., Suite 101, Līhuʻe, HI 96766, tel. 800/262–1400, www.kauaivisitorsbureau.org).

HAMURA SAIMIN SHOP, LĪHUʻE (4G)
Original Fast Food, p. 44

The shop opens at 10 AM and closes when business slows down, sometimes 10 PM or as late as 2 AM on weekends. All over the state you can find diners, stands, takeout counters, *okazuya*s (Japanese lunch stands), and small restaurants that sell local food—individually defined and drawing from a wide multicultural mix of cuisines—to local people. Typical of the style is the "mixed plate"—start with scoops of white rice and macaroni salad, then add whatever you like: Portuguese sausage, Hawaiian pig, Korean ribs, Japanese teriyaki, or Spam, a big favorite in Hawaii. In some of the best eateries, the menu hasn't changed much since the owner's great-grandparents started the business. Often the building (if there is one) hasn't changed much either. Also look for authentic local food at community festivals and fairs.

CONTACT: Hamura Saimin Shop, 2956 Kress St., downtown Līhuʻe, tel. 808/245–3271.

LODGING: Just 8 mi north of Līhuʻe, **Kauaʻi Coconut Beach Resort,** with a lobby waterfall that drops two stories, provides the full Hawaiian experience, down to the poolside bar, nightly lūʻaus, and ample, island-decor rooms that mostly look out on the ocean. Box 830, Kapaʻa, HI 96746, tel. 808/760–8555, 808/822–3455, or 800/222–5642, fax 808/822–1830, www.kcb.com. 312 rooms. Beach, pool, restaurant, lounge, 3 tennis courts. From $150.

OPTIONS: Elsewhere on Kauaʻi, look for the **Kalāheo Coffee Company & Cafe** and the **Lāwaʻi Restaurant** (both 4G). In the Waikīkī area (4C) of Oʻahu, go to Kapahulu Avenue for the **Rainbow Drive-In** or **Ono Hawaiian Food.** On the Big Island, visit the decidedly uncontemporary **Ocean View Inn,** on the bay in Kailua (12I), or have lunch at the **Manago Hotel** in Captain Cook (12J). In Hilo (16H), the locals crowd into the **Hilo Lunch Shop** for takeout, **Honu's Nest** has the town talking, and **Ocean Sushi Deli** is a popular tiny takeout shop. On Maui's west side, go to the old **Honolua Store** in Kapalua (8C); even more antique is **Kitadas** in the Upcountry town of Makawao (10D). Wailuku (9D) offers the most choices for this type of eating: try **Sam Sato's** on Wili Pa Loop. At Hāna

Bay (11D), try to connect with one of the irregular appearances of **Uncle Bill's** mobile lunch wagon. On Moloka'i, just start eating.

KALALAU TRAIL, NĀ PALI COAST (3F)
The Heart of Lightness, p. 72

The trail is best (driest) between May and September. Park your car at the end of Hwy. 56 and start walking. Most hikers settle for the rough but invigorating 2 mi to Hanakāpī'ai stream, then come home. The backpacker's option to Hanakoa or the full 11 mi to the wilderness campground at Kalalau Beach requires a state permit, limited to five nights. Nature is your only amenity: you bathe in a waterfall and filter your drinking water out of a stream.

CONTACT: Hawai'i Division of State Parks, Box 167, Līhu'e, HI 96766, tel. 808/274–3446. Register if you plan to hike past Hanakāpī'ai. For camping permits, plan a year in advance.

DISTANCES: Road's end is 40 mi northwest of Līhu'e.

LODGING: Hanalei Colony Resort is a 5-acre beachfront property near the end of the Hā'ena road. No TVs or phones in these 2-bedroom suites with lanais; the emphasis is on peace. Box 206, Hā'ena, HI 96714, tel. 808/826–6235 or 800/628–3004, fax 808/826–9893, www.hcr.com. 52 suites with kitchens. Pool, hot tub, laundry. From $145. Between the trail and Līhu'e is **Kapa'a Sands,** with two-story condo buildings right on the beach, amid meticulously landscaped grounds bursting with flowers and just a walk from shops and restaurants. 380 Papaloa Rd., Kapa'a, HI 96746, tel. 808/822–4901 or 800/222–4901, fax 808/822–1556, www.kapaasands.com. 24 apts with kitchen, TV, phone. Beach, pool. $95–$143; 3-night minimum in low season, 7 nights mid-Dec.–mid-Mar.

OPTIONS: You can also appreciate the beauty of the Nā Pali Coast from the water by kayak with **Kayak Kaua'i** (tel. 808/826–9844 or 800/437–3507; tours or rentals) or by catamaran with **Nā Pali EcoAdventures** (tel. 808/826–6804 or 800/659–6804). The most stamina-testing trek in the state is the minimum-**three-day hike** to the summit of Mauna Loa

on the Big Island that starts off the access road from Saddle Road; other tough hikes start from road's end at Hilina Pali. On Maui, the hike into **Haleakal**ā **Crater** is a day well spent (see "Doing the Crater," p. 46). The epic version of the hike is to exit the crater via Kaupō Gap and keep going downhill; you'll need someone to fetch you at the bottom. Strong hikers can get from the summit to the sea in a rigorous day, but it's tough on the knees. Even if you're a hiking maniac, consider buying the guidance of local specialists. On the Big Island, go with **Hawai'i Forest & Trail** (see Options in "The Tallest Mountain on Earth," p. 83); on Maui, **Hike Maui** (tel. 808/879–5270) has extremely well informed hike leaders; on Moloka'i, the **Hā**lawa **Falls and Cultural Hike** (tel. 808/553–4355 after 5 PM) will take you into a wild valley (8C) to swim in the pool beneath a waterfall.

NATIONAL TROPICAL BOTANICAL GARDEN (4G, 4F)
Kingdom of Leaves, p. 54

The National Tropical Botanical Garden has four gardens in Hawai'i, including the 100-acre Allerton Garden on Kaua'i, the adjacent 252-acre McBryde Garden, and 1,000-acre Limahuli Garden and Preserve on Kaua'i's north shore. Visits to Allerton and McBryde are by guided tour only, which meet at the visitor center across from the Spouting Horn parking lot (Lāwa'i Bay, near Po'ipū). Limahuli (near the end of Hwy. 56, at Hā'ena) contains important collections of native medicinal plants and rare and endangered species, and can be visited with or without a tour.

CONTACT: National Tropical Botanical Garden, 3530 Papalina Rd., Kalāheo, HI 96741, tel. 808/332–7324, www.ntbg.org.

DISTANCES: From Līhu'e, 14 mi southwest to Allerton and McBryde, 40 mi northwest to Limahuli.

TOURS: Allerton Garden: Open Tues.–Sat. for 2½-hour guided tours at 9, 10, 1, and 2; cost: $30. McBryde Garden: Open Mon. for 2½-hour guided tours at 9 and 1; cost: $30. Reservations required for both: tel. 808/742–2623. Limahuli Garden: Open Tues.–Fri. and Sun. 9:30–4 for self-guided tours ($10) or 2- to 2½-hour guided tours ($15; reservations required: tel. 808/826–1056).

LODGING: Gloria's Spouting Horn Bed & Breakfast is a romantic beachside getaway near Allerton Garden. This beautifully crafted wooden home provides rooms with canopy beds, Hawaiian quilts, luxurious baths with Japanese soaking tubs, and private lanais facing the sea. Hammocks swing between coconut trees by the pool. 4464 Lāwaʻi Beach Rd., Kōloa, HI 96756, tel./fax 808/742–6995, www.glorias-bedandbreakfast.com. 3 rooms with wet bar, refrigerator, microwave, phone, TV. $250–$275, with full breakfast. Book well in advance for the well-priced **Kōloa Landing Cottages**, with spacious, simple rooms a 10-minute walk from the beach. 2704-B Hoʻonani Rd., Kōloa, HI 96756, tel. 808/742–1470 or 800/779–8773, www.koloa-landing.com. 5 cottages with full kitchen, phones. $70–$125.

OPTIONS: Another NTBG site is 122-acre **Kahanu Garden** (11D) (ʻUlaʻino Rd., tel. 808/248–8912, fax 808/248–7210) on Maui's Hāna Coast, dedicated to the study of the ethnobotany of the Pacific. As a bonus, the property—with taro fields and pandanus forests—includes Piʻilanihale Heiau (see Options in "Written in Stone," p. 87). On the Big Island, just north of Hilo, the 4-mi Scenic Route starting at Pāpaʻikou (16H) leads past moss-carpeted bridges, towering trunks, vine-draped palms, and gurgling waters to the **Hawaiʻi Tropical Botanical Garden** (27–717 Old Mamalahea Hwy., tel. 808/964–5233, fax 808/964–1338, www.htbg.com), a 17-acre rain-forest preserve with trails offering waterfalls, a lily pond with koi, and a view of beautiful Onomea Bay. On Oʻahu, across from Waimea Bay Beach Park (2A), 1,800-acre **Waimea Valley Adventure Park** (Rte. 99, tel. 808/638–8511, www.atlantisadventures.com; open daily 10–5:30; admission $24, $12 ages 4–12) has 36 gardens and thousands of species of tropical plants, exotic birds, well-preserved ruins, and even cliff-diving demonstrations.

TARO FIELDS, HANALEI (4F)

The Good Mud, p. 60

Visitors can't help but say wow when they reach the scenic viewpoint on Kauaʻi's Kūhiō Highway, just west of the Princeville turnoff. These fields, cut through by the shimmering Hanalei River, are part of working farms, as well as part of the Hanalei National Wildlife Refuge, a habitat for Hawaiʻi's endangered seabirds. The weeklong Hanalei Taro Festival, including a celebrity-chef taro-cooking contest, is held in October of even-numbered years.

CONTACT: W. T. Haraguchi Farm, Box 427, Hanalei, HI 96714, tel. 808/826–6202.

DISTANCES: 30 mi north of Līhuʻe.

LODGING: Hanalei Bay Resort—16 buildings on a cliff overlooking the bay and the north shore—is the anchor property for Kauaʻi's most elegant development, Princeville. Box 220, Hanalei, HI 96722, tel. 808/826–6522 or 800/827–4427, fax 808/826–6680, www.hanaleibayresort.com/accommodations.html. 161 rooms with minifridge, 75 suites with kitchens. Restaurant, golf course, 4 tennis courts, pool, hot tub. Rooms from $170; suites from $320, with full breakfast.

OPTIONS: Other islands also have beautiful taro regions, and taro festivals that include Hawaiian food, performances, and crafts. On Maui's popular drive to Hāna (11E), where the **East Maui Taro Festival** takes place each March, look for a viewpoint near mile marker 17 and another just past the mile 20 lookout over the fields of the Keʻanae Peninsula and the Wailua Valley. The Big Island's taro heartland—where the **Hāmākua Taro Festival** is held each November—is the Waipiʻo Valley (13G), at the end of Hwy. 240 and inaccessible except on foot or by four-wheel-drive. (Ask the tourist offices about both festivals.) On Oʻahu in August, the Windward Community College in Kāneʻohe (4B) has a one-day **Pacific Islands Taro Festival** (tel. 808/235–7433).

KAUAʻI HIGHLIGHTS

Kauaʻi's main attraction is the near-stupefying beauty of its beaches, most of them backdropped with jungle. Many of these are clustered on the north shore. Two of the best: Kēʻē Beach (3F) at road's end, with its turquoise lagoon, and Lumahaʻi Beach (4F), featured in the movie *South Pacific*. In the sunny south, the resort district of Poʻipū (4G) is rich with beaches, and the old town of Kōloa (4G), nearby, is fun to explore. The drive to Kōkeʻe State Park (3F) gives views of the "Grand Canyon of the

Pacific"—3,000-foot-deep **Waimea Canyon** (3F–G)—and provides access to several trails. One of these goes into the **Alaka'i Swamp**, an immense bog/forest that's home to Hawai'i's rarest birds. Kaua'i's big rivers—Hanalei, Hanapēpē, Hulē'ia, Wailua, and Waimea—offer blissful opportunities for lazy **kayaking**.

LĀNA'I

Little Lāna'i, a world unto itself, has taken to dubbing itself "The Secluded Isle." Once the site of the world's largest pineapple plantation, Lāna'i opened its arms to tourism in 1991 with the opening of two sensuous resorts by the company that owns the entire island. Most of the population is centered in Lāna'i City, an old plantation town of tiny, colorful houses with tin roofs and tidy gardens surrounding a park lined with a few shops, banks, and eateries. To visitors, the island offers a beach with pristine waters great for snorkeling, some unique outdoor attractions, and most of all solitude. Though most people arrive by plane, Lāna'i is the only Hawaiian island with a regular ferry service: Expeditions Lahaina-Lāna'i Passenger Ferry (Box 10, Lahaina, HI 96767, tel. 808/661–3756) makes five round-trips every day from Maui's Lahaina Harbor. The nicest way to get here, though, is with Trilogy Excursions (tel. 808/661–4743, 800/874–2666, or 888/MAUI-800, fax 808/667–7766, www.maui.net/~trilogy), a Lahaina-based company offering snorkel/dive cruises on beautiful catamarans that anchor on Lāna'i and include great lunches at Mānele Bay. For more on Lāna'i, contact Destination Lāna'i (Box 700, Lāna'i City, HI 96763, tel. 808/565–7600 or 800/947–4774, fax 808/565–9316, www.visitlanai.net).

KAUNOLŪ (7E)
Written in Stone, p. 26

The center of ancient Hawaiian life—politically, spiritually, and intellectually—was the *heiau* (pronounced "hay-ow"), a temple built in a strategic location where people could survey the landscape and study the heavens and temple "priests,"

or *kahuna*s, could commune with the gods. Though almost completely in ruins now, heiaus are held in reverence by contemporary Hawaiians, who consider it sacrilegious to stand on top of one or even disturb its stones.

CONTACT: For vehicle rental: Lāna'i City Service, tel. 808/565–7227 or 800/533–7808.

DISTANCES: Mānele Bay is 7 mi southeast of Lāna'i City; offroading begins 3 mi past the bay, before the intersection with Mānele Road.

LODGING: The **Mānele Bay Hotel,** one of Lāna'i's two luxury resorts, sits amid luxuriant gardens above a natural marine preserve, Hulopo'e Bay. Amenities include an award-winning, Jack Nicklaus—designed golf course and a six-court tennis complex with pro. The Lāna'i Co., Box 310, Lāna'i City, HI 96763, tel. 808/565–7700 or 800/321–4666, fax 808/565– 3868, www.lanai-resorts.com. 222 rooms, 27 suites, with TV, phone, A/C, minibar. Beach, pool, fitness center, game room, snorkeling, scuba, evening entertainment. From $350. You won't find much competition for the island owners' stiff resort rates, but see Lodgings in "Riding the Rim," p. 88.

OPTIONS: On all the islands you can find the ghostly remains of a proud aboriginal culture. The Big Island has done a superior job of preserving its sites. **Pu'uhonua o Hōnaunau National Historic Park** (12J) (Hwy. 160, 3½ mi from jct. with Hwy. 11; tel. 808/328–2326) in the Kona coffee-growing area is the most vivid because it's been partially restored, with thatched buildings and carved wooden images of the Hawaiian deities. **Lapakahi State Historic Park** (12G), 12 mi north of Kawaihae on Hwy. 270 (tel. 808/882–7995), is an entire village site, with an easy self-guided-tour map and exhibits showing how ancient Hawaiians fished, farmed, gathered salt, and played games. On Maui, **Kahanu Garden** (see Options in "Kingdom of Leaves," pp. 85–86) has the largest ancient monument in the state, **Pi'ilanihale Heiau** ('Ula'ino Rd., 1½ gravelly mi from the jct. with Hāna Hwy.; closed weekends; guided tour by reservation, tel. 808/248–8912). The evidence of the Wailua Valley's former status as a center of culture and power is still visible in a series of heiaus and oth-

ESCAPE TO HAWAI'I

87

er sacred sites that stretch from the ocean to Kaua'i's summit at Mount Wai'ale'ale (4F). **'Ili'ili'ōpa'e Heiau** on Moloka'i is a football field long, the second largest after Maui's. Climb the hill directly behind it to clearly see its strategic positioning. To get there, park on the Kamehameha V Hwy. 15 mi east of Kaunakakai (7C) (between mile markers 15 and 16) and take the shady five-minute hike. For courtesy, call the landowners first (tel. 808/ 558–8132). In Honolulu (3C), the **Bishop Museum** (1525 Bernice St., tel. 808/848–4129, www.bishop.hawaii.org) is the definitive collector and interpreter of all things ancient Hawaiian.

THE MUNRO TRAIL, LĀNA'IHALE (8D)
Riding the Rim, p. 68

This 8-mi dirt road takes about two hours to traverse in a four-wheel-drive vehicle. It makes a good all-day hike, too. Hikers should have raincoats and anticipate muddy conditions at the north end of the trail, in the hills behind the Lodge at Kō'ele. Because the road here at this end can be wet and somewhat slippery, you'd best make it your downhill portion. Begin the drive in the south by taking Palawai Road from Hwy. 440 and following it into the hills; when the pavement stops, just keep going.

CONTACT: For vehicle rentals: Lāna'i City Service, tel. 808/565–7227 or 800/533–7808.

DISTANCES: The off-road trip begins 2.3 mi south of Lāna'i City. The trail hits pavement again at the Lodge at Kō'ele, ½ mi from Lāna'i City.

LODGING: The trail is easy to access from **The Lodge at Kō'ele,** a luxurious perch in the cool highlands with numerous amenities, including fourposter beds, stone fireplaces, croquet on the lawn, an outstanding restaurant, and a spectacular championship golf course. The Lāna'i Co., Box 310, Lāna'i City, HI 96763, tel. 808/565–7300 or 800/321–4666, fax 808/565–3868, www.lanai-resorts.com. 92 rooms, 10 suites, with TV, phone, minibar. Stables, pool, fitness center, golf course, 3 tennis courts, shops, restaurant, tearoom, bar, evening entertainment. From $375. Or go the B&B route with

Dreams Come True, a large plantation house with beautiful gardens. (The owners also manage several rental houses.) 547 12th St., Lāna'i City, HI 96763, tel. 808/565–6961 or 800/566–6961, fax 808/565–7056, www.go-native.com/Inns/0117.html. 3 rooms. $98.50.

LĀNA'I HIGHLIGHTS

Hulopo'e Bay (7E) is a marine sanctuary and superb snorkeling spot where you can snorkel among turtles and spinner dolphins. With a Jeep you can explore other of the island's off-road features: drive the 12-mi road west from Kō'ele (7D) past the weird rust-red rock formations of the **Garden of the Gods** to wild **Polihua Beach,** whose sand rarely feels the print of a foot; or take the other route, Keōmuku Road, which drops down the windward slope to **Shipwreck Beach** (7D)—named for the rusting hulk of a supply ship stuck on the reef—where you can wander like a castaway. (Neither beach is safe for swimming.)

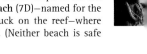

MAUI

A diversity of terrains and climates is found on Maui, the second-largest Hawaiian island—really two islands joined by a broad valley. The West Maui Mountains are old and weathered, rising up from the central plain carpeted with sugarcane fields. East Maui consists of 10,000-foot-high Haleakalā, the sleeping sister to the Big Island giants visible across the channel, with meadowy slopes that pasture horses and nurture grapevines for island wine. At the eastern edge, around the town of Hāna, is rain forest. Most visitors end up along the glorious leeward coast at or near Maui's three planned resort communities—Ka'anapali and Kapalua on West Maui and Wailea, adjoining the town of Kīhei, on the dry slopes of Haleakalā—with their luxury hotels, shops, and restaurants. Put a visitor on that shore—one who's just fled six inches of snow—add a gorgeous beach, the sun setting behind Lāna'i, a humpback whale breaching (in winter), and a pink cocktail with a paper parasol sticking out of it, and you've got a winning combination. Tourism is

booming, and with a new arts center, aquarium, modish shopping centers, and traffic problems, the island has grown some of the sophistication you won't find anywhere else in the islands but in Honolulu. Most people fly into Kahului Airport, on the central plain. Island-hopping planes land at West Maui's Kapalua Airport and at the little strip in Hāna. For more, contact the Maui Visitors Bureau (1727 Wili Pa Loop, Wailuku, HI 96793, tel. 808/244–3530 or 800/525-MAUI, www.visitmaui.com).

IN CELEBRATION OF CANOES, LAHAINA (8D)
The Pride of the Race, p. 22

The rekindling of canoe culture began in 1975 with the successful launch of the *Hokuleʻa,* a re-creation of the great two-hulled canoes the ancient Hawaiians used for oceanic exploration. *Hokuleʻa* has sailed throughout the Pacific, a symbol not only of rising Hawaiian pride but also of collaboration among Polynesian cultures. The Lahaina festival spans a two-week period in late May, filled with cultural events, performances, exhibits, classes, the parade, and finally a ceremonial launching followed by a lūʻau. In a way, Front Street in Lahaina—once Hawaiʻi's capital—sees a parade every day: the informal pageant of tourists streaming along the narrow sidewalks of this old whaling town, past the T-shirt shops and galleries, buildings from the missionary era, and eateries pumping with glad noise.

CONTACT: Lahaina Town Action Committee, 648 Wharf St., 102, Suite Lahaina, HI 96761, tel. 808/667–9175, www.visitlahaina.com. Or tel. 808/667–9194 or 888/310–1117.

DISTANCES: 27 mi from Kahului Airport.

LODGING: The **Plantation Inn,** in the heart of town and a block from the ocean, boasts a great French restaurant, Gerard's, and French provincial–flavored rooms, with floral wallpapers, brass fittings, antiques, and pull-chain toilets. 174 Lahainaluna Rd., Lahaina, HI 96761, 808/667–9225 or 800/433–6815, fax 808/667–9293, www.theplantationinn.com. 19 rooms with A/C, TV, most with patios. Pool. From $125, with breakfast. Across the street is the beautifully restored, intimate **Lahaina Inn,** warmly furnished with oriental carpets and dark wood glowing in the light of antique lamps. 127 Lahainaluna Rd., Lahaina, HI 96761, tel. 808/661–0577 or 800/669–3444, fax 808/667–9480, www. lahainainn.com. 9 rooms, 3 suites, with A/C, phones. $99–$159, with breakfast.

OPTIONS: When it's in dry dock, you can visit *Hokuleʻa* at Honolulu's (3C) Hawaiʻi Maritime Center (Ala Moana Blvd., Pier 7, tel. 808/536–6373). Experience what it was like to crew one of these voyaging canoes with an excursion on the *Ka Ha O Kanaloa* (beach at Kāʻanapali [8D], 3 mi north of Lahaina, tel. 808/876–1111), including a cultural presentation and paddling instructions. Every island has outrigger-canoe clubs whose members practice and compete vigorously; watch for **regattas**—and their visitor-friendly beach parties—on weekends May through September.

LŪʻAU, LAHAINA (8D)
Live Like a Hawaiian, p. 8

The best lūʻau is always the one that happens next door. Perhaps it's somebody's first birthday—in Hawaiʻi, cause for a party that lasts all weekend and occupies a small village. If you don't live next door to a bunch of Hawaiians, try a commercial lūʻau—a lot stagier than somebody's auntie improvising a hula in the backyard, but wonderful fun.

MAUI: For a great show in a beachside setting, do the nightly **Old Lahaina Lūʻau,** near Mala Wharf (tel. 808/667–1998; $65). For an innovative twist, try **The Feast at Lele** (505 Front St., Lahaina, tel. 808/667–5353 or 808/661–8399; Tues., Thurs., Sat. eves; $89), served in five courses, each a gourmet tribute to a different Pacific island culture; the setting is intimate, and the show is exciting.

KAUAʻI: The island's best and showiest lūʻau is at the **Kauaʻi Coconut Beach Resort** (Kapaʻa, tel. 808/822–3455, ext. 651, or 800/222–5642, fax 808/822–1830, www.kcb.com; nightly 6–9; $55). The **Tahiti Nui Lūʻau** (Kuhio Hwy., Hanalei, tel. 808/826–6277; Wed. eve; $40) is a small event that's pretty close to a family party—and a rambunctious one at that.

OʻAHU: For the ultimate Waikīkī Beach version, try the one at the palatial **Royal Hawaiian Hotel** (2259 Kalākaua Ave., tel.

808/923–7311, www.royal-hawaiian.com; Mon. eve; $78). For the biggest blowout—a Hollywood-style production with a huge cast of college kids that draws busloads of tourists—reserve a place at the **Polynesian Cultural Center** (55–370 Kamehameha Hwy., Lā'ie, tel. 808/293–3333 or 800/367–7060, www.polynesianculturalcenter.com; Mon.–Sat. eves; $95), an hour north of Honolulu.

BIG ISLAND: For a time-traveling illusion of old Polynesia, head for the lū'au at **Kona Village Resort** (6 mi north of the Kona airport, Kailua-Kona, tel. 808/325–5555 or 800/367–5290, fax 808/325–5124, www.konavillage.com; Fri. eve; $69.75), a village of thatched shelters around a jungle lagoon with no sign of civilization.

SUMMIT, HALEAKALĀ NATIONAL PARK (10–11D–E)
Doing the Crater, p. 46

Twenty-seven miles of hiking trails run through the crater's diverse micro-universe, linking the Bottomless Pit, Pele's Paint Pot, and other monstrosities with three cabins and two campgrounds. Ideally, do the crater as an all-day trek. Start at the summit, hiking down Sliding Sands Trail, crossing the crater floor, then working your way back out by means of the Halemau'u switchbacks. You'll emerge at the 8,000-foot level, 20 minutes' drive from where you started, so it's best to park your car at the Halemau'u trailhead and hitch to the summit. Nonhikers can drive to the summit, stopping off at overlooks with views into the crater, and on the way down, check out a botanical garden and a cattle ranch with a unique winery (see "Tropical Cowboys," p. 62 and below). There's a 24-hour glass-enclosed lookout at the top with a 360-degree view. The 27,284-acre national park has a visitor center at 7,000 feet, open daily 7:30–4.

CONTACT: Haleakalā National Park, Box 369, Makawao, HI 96768, tel. 808/572–4400 or 808/572–9306, www.nps.gov/halehale.htm, for details on camping and guided hikes. To check on sunrise times and park weather conditions, which can be severe, call 808/871–5054.

PRICES: Admission $10.

LODGING: The park maintains three **cabins** inside the crater. Each has a woodstove, a propane stove, 12 bunks, potable water, and a pit toilet. Each month the cabins are assigned by lottery to those whose requests in writing are received at least two months before the first day of the month in question. Tents can be pitched (with permit; first come, first served) by a couple of the cabins, and there are toilets and drinking water. The **Hosmer Grove** campground (no permit), a lovely forested area a mile from the park entrance, has six sites, pit toilets, drinking water, and cooking shelters. There's no "Crater Hotel" anywhere near the park, but to feel close to the spirit of the mountain, try a B&B in the Upcountry area, like the **Maui Golden Bamboo Ranch,** with restored old ranch buildings at the edge of the rain forest. 422 Kaupakalua Rd., Ha'iku, HI 96708, tel. 808/572–7824 or 800/344–1238, fax 808/572–7824, www.goldenbamboo.com. 1 studio, 2 suites, 1 cottage, with kitchen, phone, TV, CD player. $85–$95, with breakfast. **Hale Ho'okipa Inn** is a lovingly restored, hand-crafted home c. 1924, furnished with antiques. 32 Pakani Pl., Makawao, HI 96768, tel. 808/572–6698, fax 808/573–2580, www.supak.com/mauibnb. 3 rooms, 1 suite, with TV. $60–$135, with breakfast.

OPTIONS: Pony Express Tours (tel. 808/667–2200 or 808/878–6698, www.maui.net/~ponex/index.html) has various trail rides, including an excursion on horseback into the crater, or see it from above with **Blue Hawaiian Helicopter** (tel. 808/871–8844, 808/961–5600, or 800/745–BLUE, www.bluehawaiian.com).

'ULUPALAKUA RANCH, 'ULUPALAKUA (9E)
Tropical Cowboys, p. 62

It's a tough business raising beef on the steep slopes of a remote tropical island. To meet the financial challenges, 'Ulupalakua Ranch is learning to diversify. As a result, the ranch is becoming a very pleasant, low-key destination for visitors curious about life in Upcountry Maui—as the fertile western slopes of Haleakalā are known. The cluster of rustic buildings at ranch headquarters includes a general store selling deli goods, *paniolo* gear, and excellent Maui crafts. The free museum is in the King's Cottage, built in the 1880s for visits

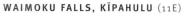

from David Kalākaua, the last king of Hawai'i. It's worth the drive just for the sprawling views of the hillside, the magnificent trees, and the glittering sea punctuated by small islands. Also here is Tedeschi Vineyards (tel. 808/878–1266, fax 808/876–0127; free tours 9:30–2:30), which produces nearly a dozen kinds of still and sparkling wine from ranch-grown grapes as well as from pineapples; the tasting room (open daily 9–5) features an 18-foot-long mango-wood bar and a selection of Maui-made gifts.

CONTACT: 'Ulupalakua Ranch, 'Ulupalakua, HI 96790, tel. 808/878–1202.

DISTANCES: 35 mi from Kahului.

LODGING: In nearby Kēōkea, the **Silver Cloud Guest Ranch** provides comfort, silence, and sweeping views. The ranch house has six guest rooms (two upstairs with seaward-looking lanais) and a big kitchen. The bunkhouse has a suite and four studios with mini-kitchens and simple but pleasant decor. The Lanai Cottage, a real treat, is a little one-bedroom house with a woodstove, a full kitchen, and a red claw-foot tub. R.R. 2, Box 201, Kula, HI 96790, tel. 808/878–6101 or 800/532–1111, fax 808/878–2132, www.silvercloudranch.com. 12 rooms. $85–$150, with full breakfast.

OPTIONS: Off-road tours from **Maui Jeep Adventures** (tel. 808/876–1177, fax 808/876–1911, www.mauijeepadventures.com; $82.29 adults, $46.88 ages 5–10) provide glimpses of the ranch's operations, including its elk herd, while teaching about the ecology and history of the area; tours include pickup service in the Wailea area. The economy no longer supports many working paniolos; Maui's are most visible on the weekend nearest the Fourth of July, when they take over the town of Makawao (10D) for an annual **parade and two-day rodeo** (tel. 808/572–2076). The Big Island is another bastion of paniolo culture; start by visiting the **Parker Ranch Visitor Center and Museum** (Parker Ranch Shopping Center, Hwy. 19, Kamuela [13G], near Waimea, tel. 808/885–7655, www.parkerranch.com), including exhibits and a video on this historic ranch. There are wonderful places to go horseback riding on every island; on Maui, try **Pony Express Tours** (see Options in "Doing the Crater," p. 90).

WAIMOKU FALLS, KĪPAHULU (11E)
The Majesty of Water, p. 40

Haleakalā National Park not only girdles the summit of the mountain but also runs downhill along wild Kīpahulu Valley and touches the sea at 'Ohe'o Gulch, site of the so-called Seven Sacred Pools. Leave your car at the park's lot and hike up the left side of the stream; the trail is clearly marked. Some basic warnings about waterfalls and streams: Watch out for submerged boulders—don't go leaping heedlessly into tempting pools. Don't drink the water. Most of all, keep an eye on the weather. When it rains up in the mountains, stream levels can rise with alarming speed and force; beware of flash flooding.

CONTACT: Haleakalā National Park, Box 369, Makawao, HI 96768, tel. 808/572–4400 or 808/572–9306. For weather conditions, call 808/871–5054.

DISTANCES: Trailhead is 13 mi south of Hāna town.

LODGING: You can camp at the park's **Kīpahulu site** in a grassy coastal field with pit toilets and barbecues (no drinking water; no open campfires; no fee or reservation for 3 nights or less). Perched between a cove in Hāna Bay and an ancient fish pond, **Hāna Hale Malamalama**—beautifully handcrafted buildings of exotic hardwoods in Pacific Rim styles—is a great nearby choice for an overnight. Box 374, Hāna, HI 96713, tel. 808/248–7718, fax 808/248–7429, www.hanahale.com. 4 suites, 2 cottages, with full kitchen, private lanai, TV/VCR, phone, some Jacuzzis. $110–$195.

OPTIONS: You can stalk the wild waterfall everywhere in Hawai'i. West Maui has the second-tallest cascade in the state, the jaw-droppingly vertical **Honokohau Falls,** but the only way to see it is by helicopter (Blue Hawaiian Helicopter, tel. 808/871–8844, 808/961–5600, or 800/745–BLUE, www.bluehawaiian.com). On Moloka'i, explore **Hālawa Valley** (8C) and its classic falls with a guide provided by Hālawa Falls and Cultural Hike (tel. 808/553–4355 after 5 PM). On the Big Island, walk through the lush, breezy, 66-acre **'Akaka Falls State Park** (15H) on the Hāmākua Coast to view two amazing cascades more than 400 feet high. Even in Honolulu a pleasant, easy waterfall hike is close at hand: the **Manoa Falls Trail** in Manoa Valley, a few miles above Waikīkī (4C). For hikes into **Moanalua Valley,** contact Moanalua Gardens (tel. 808/833–1944), a park with spreading monkeypod trees on the west side of Honolulu (3C). On Kaua'i, near Wailua (4F), you can drive to the impressive **Wailua Falls** (familiar from the opening sequences of *Fantasy Island*) on Hwy. 583 and the dramatic **'Ōpaeka'a Falls** on Hwy. 580.

MAUI HIGHLIGHTS

Most of the great beaches are along the leeward coast; don't miss **Mākena Beach State Park** (9E), south of Wailea. You can't say you've been to Maui without tripping around the historic town of **Lahaina** (8D) (see "The Pride of the Race," p. 22). The all-day rain-forest drive to the remote town of **Hāna** (11E) is essential for absorbing the full experience of life in Polynesia. **The Crater** in Haleakalā National Park (see "Doing the Crater," p. 46) is a true natural wonder. The **Maui Ocean Center** in Mā'alaea (9D) is a world-class aquarium dedicated to Pacific marine life. **Lahaina and Mā'alaea harbors** provide nearly every form of water sport you can think of, including humpback whale–watching in winter.

MOLOKA'I

The quiet, unsophisticated, somehow spiritual island of Moloka'i has only 7,000 residents, yet it counts among them more native Hawaiians than any of the other islands can boast. Community life hinges on one town, Kaunakakai, little more than a street lined with a few crowded little markets and homespun gift shops. Travelers from the mainland need to change planes in Honolulu or Kahului for the 25-minute flight to tiny Ho'olehua Airport. For more on the island, contact the Moloka'i Visitors Association (Box 960, Kaunakakai, HI 96748, tel. 808/553–3876, 800/553–0404, or 800/800–6367, fax 808/553–5288, www.molokai-hawaii.com).

DAMIEN TOURS, KALAUPAPA (7C)
Revered Outcasts, p. 30

The peninsula is a memorial to Hawai'i's lepers, banished here in the terror of infection that began in 1865; the drug treatment that arrests the disease and prevents its spread was developed in 1946. (A video at Waikīkī's Damien Museum tells the story.) Though Kalaupapa's residents guard their privacy, people 16 and older are welcome to visit for the day, provided they are guests of a resident. Damien Tours is the only company licensed to admit the public. The emotionally charged tour traverses an astonishing landscape; the guide's delivery is equal parts Will Rogers and Rodney Dangerfield. The four-hour bus ride departs from the Kalaupapa airstrip at 10:15 AM.

CONTACT: Damien Tours, c/o Kalaupapa Settlement, Kalaupapa, HI 96742, tel. 808/567–6171.

DISTANCES: From Kaunakakai, 11 mi north to trailhead.

PRICES: $40.

LODGINGS: In keeping with the down-to-earth spirit of the island, **Hotel Moloka'i** offers accommodations in simple, Polynesian-style buildings on the beach near Kaunakakai; spring for the upstairs ocean-view rooms. The oceanfront restaurant—about the only good one on the island—has Hawaiian entertainment poolside. Mile Marker 2, Kamehameha V Hwy., Box 546, Kaunakakai, HI 96748, tel. 808/553–5347, fax 808/553–5047, www.hotelmolokai.com. 37 rooms, most with king and two twin beds, lanai, minifridge, TV, phone; some kitchenettes. Pool, shop. $78–$133.

OPTIONS: From Maui, **Paragon Air** (tel. 808/244–3356 or 800/428–1231, www.maui.net/~wings/index.html) will set up the whole experience. **Moloka'i Mule Ride** (tel. 808/567–6088 or 800/567–7550, evenings 808/567–6400, fax 808/567–6244, www.muleride.com) will get you from O'ahu or Maui onto the back of a reliable mule, down the trail, onto the Damien Tours bus, then, four hours later, back home—an amazing day. Or you can **walk** the steep, 3.8-mi, 26-switchback trail (starts at Pālā'au State Park on Hwy. 470, 7 mi north of Ho'olehua Airport). If you start by 8 AM you'll be down on the peninsula in time to meet the bus. Make a reservation with Damien Tours, and pack your own lunch.

KA HULA PIKO FESTIVAL, KALUAKO'I (6C)
Born Again, p. 66

Hula—a dance of graceful movements, spiritual and layered with meaning—kept alive the history, traditions, and genealogy of the islanders. Passed down by revered teachers, it preserved without a written language the culture of the ancient peoples. In the 19th century, missionaries persuaded their royal converts to ban the dance as immoral, but David Kalākaua, the "Merrie Monarch" who reigned until 1891, revived it. Moloka'i's festival takes place each May at Pāpōhaku Beach County Park, at the west end of the island. A week of music, dance, lectures, crafts, and storytelling culminates in the *ho'olaule'a*, or shindig, on the third Saturday of the month. Plan ahead; the island's few accommodations fill up.

CONTACT: Moloka'i Visitors Association, see above.

DISTANCES: 22 mi west of Kaunakakai.

LODGING: The natural choice at the festival's remote location is **Kaluako'i Hotel & Golf Club,** an aging but still elegant beachside property. Small, simple rooms are in two dozen two-story units surrounded by vast lawns and flowering shrubs everywhere you look. Box 1977, Maunaloa, HI 96770, tel. 808/552–2555 or 888/552–2550, fax 808/552–2821, www.kaluakoi.com. 104 rooms with TV/VCR, fridge, private lanai, some kitchens. Restaurant, bar, pool, shops, tennis courts, golf course and pro. From $100.

OPTIONS: The biggest hula gathering is the much-publicized and annually televised **Merrie Monarch Festival** (Hawai'i Naniloa Hotel, 93 Banyan Dr., Hilo, HI 96720, tel. 808/935–9168, www.hotspots.hawaii.com/hula.html), which takes place on the Big Island the first week after Easter; reserve accommodations and tickets at least a year in advance. Since 1937 visitors have enjoyed the free **Kodak Hula Show** in the Waikīkī Shell at Kapi'olani Park in Honolulu (3C) (tel. 808/627–3379, www.kodak.com/cluster/global/en/consumer/events/hulashows.html; Tues.–Thurs. 10 AM, weather permitting). The art of hula is practiced throughout Hawai'i, and it's a rare week that passes without some opportunity to see a performance somewhere; to find one, check the local paper or call one of the tourist offices.

MOLOKA'I HIGHLIGHTS
You can tour the whole island by car in a single day. The west end includes **Pāpōhaku Beach** (6C), the largest white-sand beach in the state. The east end is dotted with wild little beaches and coves before the road ends at gorgeous **Hālawa Valley** (8C), with its sinuous bay and 2-mi hike to 250-foot **Moa'ula Falls**. Central Moloka'i's lee shore is lined with a system of huge fish ponds constructed in ancient times, and the main town of **Kaunakakai** (7C) is here. The route north includes the **Moloka'i Museum and Cultural Center** (in a preserved old sugar mill), overlooks of the island's seacliffs at **Pālā'au State Park** (7C), and remote **Mo'omomi Beach** (6C), a good place for surfing, fishing, or ambling along the shore. A wagon ride (tel. 808/558–8380) through mango and coconut groves takes you to 'Ili'ili'ōpa'e **Heiau** (see Options in "Written in Stone," pp. 87–88).

O'AHU

The name is said to mean "gathering place." How prophetic, for 80% of the state's population lives here. Most people inhabit the capital city, Honolulu, bracketed on one side by the military installations at Pearl Harbor (some buildings are still marked by strafings received on December 7, 1941) and on the other by the famous profile of Diamond Head crater. There's nothing else like Honolulu in the Pacific—a big, beautiful, multiethnic city that still manages to retain a sense of neighborhoods, of Hawaiian culture, and of Polynesian informality. By contrast, the outlying and windward areas feel much like the rustic outer islands. A two-lane highway traces most of the coast, passing through famous surf country (Waimea Bay, Sunset Beach, and the Banzai Pipeline) along the north shore. O'ahu lacks any single volcanic peak. Instead, it's formed of two parallel mountain ranges,

Ko'olau and Wai'anae, that give the island its characteristic look: pleated walls of vertical greenery. For more information, contact the O'ahu Visitors Bureau (733 Bishop St., Honolulu, HI 96813, tel. 877/525–6248, www.visit-oahu.com).

CHINATOWN, HONOLULU (3C)
Dried Sea Cucumbers & Leis, p. 58

The only way to comprehend this dozen-block historic district is in the details—in other words, on foot, walking the narrow sidewalks and sticking your head into the shops. Get rid of your car in the parking garage at Smith Street between Pauahi and Beretania. From there walk a block or so to the corner of Hotel and Maunakea. On the ground floor of the landmark Wo Fat building, with its pagoda-style roof, you'll find the M.P. Lei Shop (tel. 808/531–3206). From here explore Maunakea Marketplace, a pedestrian mall lined with shops, including the Ying Leong Look Funn Factory (tel.808/537–4304). Hong Fa Market (115 Hotel St., tel.808/536–5521) is a small, friendly place with time to answer your questions about the exotic Asian products. Right next door, eat dim sum or order from an expansive menu at the two-story Sea Fortune Restaurant (tel. 808/538–6366).

LODGING: See other O'ahu listings.

OPTIONS: If you exit Chinatown on King Street heading east, you're just blocks from the **capitol district,** whose buildings represent the heart of the Kingdom of Hawai'i at its peak. The centerpiece is the grand, or grandiose, **'Iolani Palace** (tel. 808/522–0832), completed in 1882 for King David Kalākaua. Other highlights include the palatial **Ali'iolani Hale,** which houses the state Supreme Court; the odd, volcano-shaped **State Capitol;** and Georgian-style **Washington Place,** the governor's official residence.

HANAUMA BAY, KOKO HEAD (4C)
A Floating World, p. 12

An estimated 2 million people a year come to Hanauma for the sea-life immersion experience—this is, after all, a state park with ideal snorkeling conditions inside a clean, calm

bowlful of reef. Such heavy use would seem inconsistent with the bay's designation as a marine preserve, but the state is trying to manage the site with lifeguards, signs, free tours, and a trolley that runs between the upper parking lot and the beach. Arrive early. The park is open from 6 AM to 7 PM every day except Tuesday.

CONTACT: Hanauma Bay Nature Park 24-hour info: tel. 808/396–4229. Equipment rentals: tel. 808/395–4725.

DISTANCES: 10 mi east of Waikīkī.

PRICES: $1 per vehicle and $3 per person; $6 for rental of mask, fins, and snorkel.

LODGING: Set in a serene, lush valley just a few minutes from the hubbub of Honolulu is the **Mānoa Valley Inn,** a fully restored 1919 Victorian listed on the National Register of Historic Places. The rooms, including a billiard den, are filled with period antiques. 2001 Vancouver Dr., Honolulu, HI 96822, tel. 808/947–6019 or 800/634–5115, fax 808/946–6168, www.aloha.net/~wery. 7 large suites and 1 cottage, with Continental breakfast on the lanai, complimentary wine and cheese. Rooms and suites $99–$190, cottage $165.

OPTIONS: You can snorkel the safer reefs (and join a scuba dive boat in any small harbor) of every Hawaiian island. Lāna'i offers one of the finest snorkeling experiences in **Hulopo'e Bay** (7E), a marine preserve visited by Hawaiian sea turtles and spinner dolphins. On Maui, snorkelers prefer the leeward beaches, such as **Honolua Bay** (8C), **Black Rock** at Kā'anapali (8D), and any of the small beaches in **Wailea** (9E); or hire a charismatic marine biologist to guide you by contacting Ann Fielding's **Snorkel Maui** (tel. 808/572–8437, www.maui.net/~annf). On Kaua'i's north shore go to **Kē'ē Beach** (3F); on the south shore try **Kōloa Landing** (4G). On the Big Island, go to the Kona side for **Kahalu'u Beach** (12I), 4½ mi south of Kailua, or **Kealakekua Bay** (12J) in coffee country (see Hawaiian Highlights, pp. 83–84). Visit sea creatures without getting wet at either of two excellent aquariums. On O'ahu, the **Waikīkī Aquarium** (4C) (tel.808/928–9741, www.otted.hawaii.edu/aquarium), run by the University of Hawai'i, sits by the shore in Queen Kapi'olani Park. The

Maui Ocean Center (Māʻalaea Harbor, 192 Māʻalaea Rd., Wailuku [9D], tel. 808/270-7000, www.coralworld.com/moc/), new in 1998, has inventive and engaging displays, including a touch pool, a Whale Discovery Center, and an acrylic tunnel through the middle of a 750-thousand-gallon tank.

WAIKĪKĪ, HONOLULU (4C)
The Beach of All Beaches, p. 36

It's not hard to get to Waikīkī Beach—everybody does it. From Honolulu, nine bus lines service the strip, or take the Waikīkī Trolley (day pass: $15). Or you can drive the coastal route along Ala Moana Boulevard, then park and explore the mile-long extravaganza on foot. On the beach you'll find lifeguards and rental surfboards, boogie boards, catamarans, and canoes.

DISTANCES: 2 mi east of downtown Honolulu.

LODGING: The **Royal Hawaiian Hotel,** built in 1927, inaugurated and continues to proclaim the grand era of Waikīkī tourism. Here, as the hotel modestly asserts, "desires are met before you're even aware of them." Even if you don't stay here, you can sit at the Mai Tai Bar with a coral-pink cocktail, look out at the beach, and know that you have truly arrived. 2259 Kalākaua Ave., Honolulu, HI 96815-2578, tel. 808/923-7311 or 800/325-3589, fax 808/924-7098, www.royal-hawaiian.com. 527 rooms and suites with A/C, TV, phone, fridge, safe, computer hookups, some private lanais. 3 restaurants, 24-hour room service, pool, private beach area, children's program, business center, 20 shops, salon, day spa. From $325. Though Waikīkī is known for its high-rises, the **Hawaiiana Hotel** offers a human-scale alternative a block from the beach. With its low-rise, 1950s-era look comes lovely Hawaiian ambiance and heartfelt aloha spirit. 260 Beach Walk, Honolulu, HI 96815, tel. 808/923-3811 or 800/367-5122, fax 808/926-5728, www.waikiki.com/travel/hotels/oahu.html. 95 rooms with A/C, TV, phone. $95–$165, including Kona coffee and pineapple juice by the pool each morning, Hawaiian entertainment two nights a week.

OPTIONS: While Waikīkī has no equal, other beach districts have their own visitor dreamlands based on the formula: luxury properties that anchor a complete visitor environment, part natural beauty and part theatrical construction of pools, gardens, restaurants, bars, and shops. Starting in the late sixties, Maui created three resort communities along the leeward shores: **Kāʻanapali** (8D), **Kapalua** (8C), and **Wailea** (9E). The Big Island is still developing resorts wherever the **Kohala Coast** provides a cove or pocket-size beach. Kauaʻi's counterpart is the 11,000-acre planned development of **Princeville** (4F), adjoining Hanalei Bay. The most extreme variation—just the property, the beach, a golf course, and blissful silence—is Lānaʻi's **Mānele Bay Hotel** (see Lodging in "Written in Stone," p. 87). Travelers who stay elsewhere should feel free to enjoy these resorts by touring the grounds, eating and drinking there, and sharing the beaches, which, throughout Hawaiʻi, are public and open places.

OʻAHU HIGHLIGHTS
Besides Chinatown and the historic district (see "Dried Sea Cucumbers & Leis," pp. 58 and 94), **Honolulu** (3C) offers the pleasures of urban life: shopping (especially at Ala Moana Center and Ward Center), museums (Bishop Museum for Hawaiiana, Honolulu Academy of Arts for Pacific Rim and world art), concert halls, nightclubs, a zoo.... **Pearl Harbor** (3C), 7 mi northwest of downtown, is the state's most visited site. The USS *Arizona* Memorial commemorates the infamous surprise attack that set off World War II in the Pacific, and the USS *Bowfin* Submarine Museum and Park pays tribute to submarine technology. You'll find beautiful **beaches and snorkeling areas** at the southeast tip near the towns of Kaneʻohe and Kailua (both 4B). For the chance (in winter) of watching some epic surf, stop at the little town of Haleʻiwa (2B) and the North Shore beaches. The **Polynesian Cultural Center** (see "Live Like a Hawaiian," p. 90) in Lāʻie is a popular theme park depicting native life of the Pacific and has a lūʻau Monday–Saturday evenings. **Waimea Valley Adventure Park** (see "Kingdom of Leaves," pp. 85–86) combines cultural and botanical sights with play-hard activities involving all-terrain vehicles, mountain bikes, and kayaks.

Fate hijacked Paul Wood's life in 1976, when a ruptured appendix turned a simple Maui vacation into a tempestuous 25-year relationship with his adopted home, Hawai'i. As a freelance journalist, newspaper columnist, commercial writer, and contributor to island and mainland periodicals, he often writes about the islands he loves. He's the author of several locally published books, including two collections of humorous pieces — *Four Wheels Five Corners: Facts of Life in Upcountry Maui* and *Forbidden Fruit Juice: Tales From the American Tropics.*

British photographer Robert Holmes launched his distinguished career covering the 1975 British Everest Expedition for the London *Daily Mail.* He has since traveled the world for major magazines including *National Geographic, Islands, Travel Holiday, Geo, Life,* and *Travel + Leisure.* Widely recognized as one of the world's foremost travel photographers, he was the first person to twice receive the Photographer of the Year Award from the Society of American Writers.